W9-CZK-507

iPad in One Hour FOR LAWYERS

BY TOM MIGHELL

ABA LAW
PRACTICE
DIVISION
The Business of Practicing Law

Commitment to Quality: The Law Practice Division is committed to quality in our publications. Our authors are experienced practitioners in their fields. Prior to publication, the contents of all our books are rigorously reviewed by experts to ensure the highest quality product and presentation. Because we are committed to serving our readers' needs, we welcome your feedback on how we can improve future editions of this book.

Cover design by RIPE Creative, Inc.

Figure 1.1, iPad Air by Zach Vega, has been edited and is licensed under Creative Commons Attribution-Share Alike 3.0 Unported license. http://creativecommons.org/licenses/by-sa/3.0/deed.en.

Figure 5.2 courtesy of Logitech.

Nothing contained in this book is to be considered as the rendering of legal advice for specific cases, and readers are responsible for obtaining such advice from their own legal counsel. This book and any forms and agreements herein are intended for educational and informational purposes only.

The products and services mentioned in this publication are under or may be under trademark or service mark protection. Product and service names and terms are used throughout only in an editorial fashion, to the benefit of the product manufacturer or service provider, with no intention of infringement. Use of a product or service name or term in this publication should not be regarded as affecting the validity of any trademark or service mark.

The Law Practice Division of the American Bar Association offers an educational program for lawyers in practice. Books and other materials are published in furtherance of that program. Authors and editors of publications may express their own legal interpretations and opinions, which are not necessarily those of either the American Bar Association or the Law Practice Division unless adopted pursuant to the bylaws of the Association. The opinions expressed do not reflect in any way a position of the Division or the American Bar Association.

Printed in the United States of America.

Library of Congress Cataloging-in-Publication Data

Mighell, Tom, author.
   iPad in one hour for lawyers / by Tom Mighell. — Third edition.
     pages cm
   Includes bibliographical references and index.
   ISBN 978-1-62722-614-1 (alk. paper)
  1. Practice of law—United States—Data processing. 2. iPad (Computer) 3. Lawyers—United States—Handbooks, manuals, etc. I. American Bar Association. Law Practice Division, sponsoring body. II. Title.
   KF320.A9M48 2014
   004.1675—dc23

                      2014006965

Discounts are available for books ordered in bulk. Special consideration is given to state bars, CLE programs, and other bar-related organizations. Inquire at Book Publishing, American Bar Association, 321 N. Clark Street, Chicago, Illinois 60654.

www.ShopABA.org

Contents

About the Author

Tom Mighell is a senior consultant with Contoural Inc., where he helps companies develop information governance programs and deal with litigation readiness and eDiscovery issues. Prior to becoming a consultant, Tom practiced as a trial lawyer for eighteen years with the firm of Cowles & Thompson in Dallas. He served as the firm's litigation technology support coordinator for six years, running the technology for lawyers in more than fifty trials.

In addition to this book, Tom is the author of *iPad in One Hour for Litigators* and *iPad Apps in One Hour for Lawyers* and the co-author (along with Dennis Kennedy) of *The Lawyer's Guide to Collaboration Tools and Technologies: Smart Ways to Work Together*, all published by the American Bar Association's Law Practice Division. Tom publishes two blogs: the legal technology blog *Inter Alia* (www.inter-alia.net) and *iPad 4 Lawyers* (http://ipad4lawyers.squarespace.com). He is also the cohost of *The Kennedy-Mighell Report*, a legal technology podcast produced by the Legal Talk Network (www.legaltalknetwork.com).

Tom has been a member of the ABA's Law Practice Management Section (now Law Practice Division) since 2003 and was inducted into the College of Law Practice Management in 2013. He served for four years on the ABA TECHSHOW Board and was chair of ABA TECHSHOW 2008. He also served as chair of the ABA's Law Practice Management Section from 2011 to 2012 and currently serves as chair of the Division's Publishing Board. Tom received both his B.A. (1987) and J.D. (1990) degrees from the University of Texas at Austin.

Acknowledgments

To Denise, Lindsay, and Laura of the fantastic LP publishing staff, for all of your expertise and dedication in publishing high-quality practice management books; to the members of the LP Publishing Board, which is without a doubt the hardest-working group of people in the entire Division; and to Kenny, who mercifully looked the other way when I bought all the iPads I needed to write this update.

Introduction

Getting Started

If you're reading this book, then either you have just purchased a new iPad or you're trying to decide whether to get one. If you're the proud owner of a new iPad, congratulations! You now own the device that started a revolution in computing. If you haven't quite decided whether to buy yet, let's see what we can do to convince you.

Although competitors offer devices built on the Android, Windows, and even BlackBerry platforms, the iPad was the first, and is still the best known, tablet on the market. Although the other platforms have some intriguing options, in this book we'll be talking all iPad, all the time.

Your iPad is a powerful device. It allows you to do many things you used to do on your laptop or desktop—surf the web, read your email, type notes or documents—but it can do much more, and it weighs only a pound. So let's get started!

About This Book

First, a quick word about the contents of this book. I only have an hour to share some quick iPad lessons, so I really need to make my time with you count. Therefore, I've tried to appeal to all types of iPad users: those of you who are tech proficient as well as those who might need a little extra help. The first few lessons are more basic, addressing the setup and overall management of your iPad. The remaining lessons cover specific ways to be productive with your iPad, including apps designed for practicing lawyers. It may take you a little more than an hour to make it through all six lessons—I hope you won't hold that against me!

In "Beyond the Lessons," I'll cover a lot of the detail I didn't include in the lessons: finger moves and shortcuts, advanced email settings, and more.

Disclosure

Before we start, a disclosure: I belong to an affiliate marketing service that pays me a very small commission on all apps sold by clicking on the links included in this book. If that's an issue for you, don't use these links; just go to Google and search for "[App name] iPad app," and you'll see a link unconnected to my affiliate account. And please rest assured that this affiliation has no bearing on the apps I mention; I have installed all of the apps I discuss here on my iPad, and I'm still using most of them on a regular basis.

Getting Started

Before you read this book, it's a good idea to make sure you've completed the following basic steps:

- **Purchase your iPad!** Hopefully you already have your iPad by the time you're ready to start these lessons. It doesn't matter whether you purchased the Wi-Fi-only or Wi-Fi/LTE version or whether you own a 16, 32, 64, or 128 GB model. You might be using an older model given to you by someone else. Unless you're using the very first iPad, released in 2010 (which is really outdated and cannot handle many of the functions of later models), the lessons apply no matter what type of iPad you own. For more on the latest iPads, see the sidebar at the end of the Introduction.

- **Install iTunes on your computer (or not).** You can use Apple's iTunes software to sync the iPad with your computer and transfer files, music, and videos to the device and back up all its data. If you haven't already, visit http://www.apple.com/itunes to download and install the iTunes software. For instructions on installing iTunes on a PC, check out this article at the For Dummies website: http://www.dummies.com/how-to/content/how-to-install-itunes-on-a-windows-pc.html. You are not required to use iTunes, however; you can also back up and sync your iPad wirelessly using iCloud. We'll cover both methods of backup and the merits of each in Lesson 4.

- **Set up your iPad with iTunes.** (If you're not using iTunes, you can skip this part.) Once you install iTunes on your computer, use the cable that came in the box to connect your iPad to the computer. Every time you connect the iPad to your computer, iTunes will automatically start. To set up your iPad or configure the synchronization settings, go to **Devices** on the left side of the computer screen. (You must connect your iPad to the computer or it will not appear in the **Devices** menu.) Select **iPad** and you'll see a number of tabs. From here you can get information about your iPad and manage what you put on it:

  - **Summary.** Basics about your iPad, including capacity, serial number, whether a new software update is available, how to restore your iPad, backup options, general options, and more

  - **Info.** Where you configure your iPad to synchronize mail, contacts, or calendars (See "Beyond the Lessons" for specific instructions on these settings.)

- **Apps.** All of the software, or applications, currently installed
  on your iPad, including a list of those that support File
  Sharing (You can manage your apps from this page.
  See Lesson 3: "Multitasking and Folders.")

- The remaining tabs allow you to configure synchronization
  options for the following:

  - ringtones
  - music
  - movies
  - TV Shows
  - podcasts
  - iTunes U
  - books
  - photos

- **Sync your iPad with iTunes.** (Skip this section if you are not
  using iTunes.) Once you have adjusted these options to your liking,
  click the **Apply** button and then press **Sync**. Your iPad will take
  care of the rest!

- **Configure your security options.** Security is a serious matter, so
  before you start using your iPad, you want to secure it in the event
  it's lost or stolen. See "Beyond the Lessons" for instructions on con-
  figuring the security settings on your new device.

- **Charge the iPad battery.** To charge the battery, connect the
  iPad to a power outlet using the included cable and the 12W
  USB power adapter. You can also connect to a high-power USB
  port with the included cable, but it might take longer to charge.
  If you do not connect to a high-power port, you may see a "Not

Charging" message; some older USB ports and accessories do not provide enough power to charge an iPad. The fastest way to charge your tablet is using the 12W adapter—even so, it will take several hours to charge the large internal battery of the iPad Air. The iPad Mini will not take as long to charge. **TIP**: Your iPad will charge faster if you put it into Airplane Mode.

- **Connect to the Internet.** If you have an iPad with cellular, it should connect automatically. To connect via Wi-Fi, follow these instructions:
  - First, make sure you're in an area with a wireless connection.
  - Press **Settings**, then **Wi-Fi**, and make sure Wi-Fi is in the **ON** position.
  - A list of available networks will appear. Select the network to which you want to connect. If the network requires a password, you'll be prompted to enter it.
  - You're connected!

- **Start buying apps.** If you're new to the iPad, you'll quickly learn that it does not use programs as you might think of them on your computer. Instead, the iPad uses *apps*, short for *applications*. These are self-contained programs specifically designed for the iPad. Your iPad comes with several default applications, but if you really want to use your new device you'll need to download apps from Apple's App Store. This book contains a sampling of some of the best iPad apps for lawyers; for a more detailed list of iPad apps that lawyers can use for work, check out my blog *iPad 4 Lawyers* (http://ipad-4lawyers.squarespace.com) or my book *iPad Apps in One Hour for Lawyers* (ABA, 2012).

Once you've completed these steps, you are ready to move on to the lessons in this book. Some of the lessons are relatively short, while others are longer. But we've got a lot to cover in just one hour. So if you're ready, let's get started!

---

iPad Air or Mini: Which Should You Buy?

At the time of this book's publication, Apple offered three iPad models: (1) the older edition iPad 2 (which is still very popular and a cheaper alternative); (2) the iPad Air, a lighter, faster version of the full-size 9.7-inch iPad; and (3) the iPad Mini with Retina Display, the smaller 7-inch option. To get the most out of your iPad experience, I recommend buying one of the new iPad Air or iPad Mini devices—they are extremely powerful and fast. The iPad Air weighs just a pound and is easily the best full-size iPad ever made. That is not to say, however, that the iPad Mini is an also-ran. In fact, the specifications for both the iPad Air and iPad Mini are *identical*; there is no functional difference between the two tablets. Size is really the only difference.

Which leads to the inevitable question: Should a lawyer use an Air or a Mini? Ultimately, the answer depends on your own preference and whether you like the larger or smaller form factor. I personally believe it is harder to be productive on the iPad Mini (in fact, I use my Mini primarily for content consumption)—a bigger screen makes it easier to get stuff done. I also think some of the legal apps—TrialPad in particular, but really any evidence presentation app—are just plain easier to use on the larger tablet.

Navigating Your iPad and Browsing the Web

I always like to start exploring a new device by understanding its features, so let's take a quick walking tour of your new iPad (see Figure 1.1).

Figure 1.1 iPad Features

A. **On/Off button.** To turn the iPad on, just press and hold the On/Off button. To turn it off, press the On/Off button until the **slide to power off** screen appears. The On/Off button will also put the iPad to sleep if you press it once.

B. **Screen Rotation Lock/Mute**. This button can do one of two things:

  1. Lock the iPad's screen rotation so it will not change when you move from Landscape to Portrait mode or vice versa

  2. Automatically mute the volume on your iPad

  To select the feature you want to enable, go to **Settings** and choose **General**, and then check off your preference under **Use Side Switch to**.

C. **Volume.** Press the top half of this switch to turn up the volume and the bottom half to turn it down. If you press the lower half for a second or two, you automatically mute the sound. You'll see a volume graphic on-screen that shows the current volume level.

D. **Headphone jack.** Plug in your earbuds or headphones here to watch videos or listen to music on the iPad's Music app or on other music apps, like Spotify or Pandora.

E. **Dock connector.** Here's where you plug in the USB cable to connect your iPad to your computer for syncing or to a power outlet for charging.

F. **Microphone.** Use this to take advantage of the iPad's dictation feature, which is available in just about every app that offers text entry (when you pull up the virtual keyboard, you'll see a micro-phone button just to the left of the space bar—press it to begin dictation). The microphone is also available to other apps that need to "listen" to what's going on.

G. **FaceTime camera.** This is the camera used by FaceTime or other video chat apps to capture your face whenever you want to talk to someone else. The **iSight camera**, which will take pictures or video of other things, is located on the back of the iPad.

H. **Speakers.** Sound is projected from the iPad here.

I. **Home button.** The only button on the front of the iPad has a few functions. First, it *always* takes you Home—to the main screen, or the first screen you see when you turn on the iPad. You can also use the Home button to move to another program: just press the button, and you'll be taken back to the screen you were last viewing, where you can tap to open another program.

The iPad's Default Apps

When you first turn on your iPad, you'll notice that it comes with several apps and features already installed. With the rollout of the iPad Air, you can get even more stock Apple apps for free. They include the following:

- **App Store.** Search for the latest apps and download them to your iPad, all with the click of a button.
- **Calendar.** Learn how to set up the calendar in Lesson 2.
- **Camera.** The iPad features a 5-megapixel camera for taking photos and videos.
- **Clock.** See the time in cities all over the world, set an alarm, or use the stopwatch and timer to keep track of elapsed time.
- **Contacts.** You'll have easy access to all your contacts—learn how to set them up in Lesson 2.
- **FaceTime.** This is a great way to make video or audio-only calls to other iPad, iPhone, or Mac users. You can even switch to the camera on the back to show people what you're seeing.
- **Game Center.** For downtime, the Game Center keeps track of

your high scores in all of your games and lets you play games with friends or anyone on the network.

- **iTunes.** Browse the iTunes store and download music, books, or videos directly to your iPad.

- **Mail.** Access your email messages here. See Lesson 2 to learn how to set up your mail.

- **Maps.** Search for addresses, get directions, and use Street View to explore locations.

- **Messages.** Send a text message for free to anyone with an iPad, iPhone, or iPod Touch.

- **Music.** This is where you can access your music, audiobooks, podcasts, and other audio files.

- **Newsstand.** Access subscriptions to certain magazines or newspapers.

- **Notes.** You can use this as a very basic note-taking app (read about better note apps in Lesson 5).

- **Photo Booth.** Use this fun application to add special effects to pictures you take.

- **Photos.** Press this button to view all the photos stored on your iPad. You can group photos into Moments and Collections, and you can share them with others via email and various social media tools.

- **Reminders.** See a basic task or to-do list or get reminders of approaching deadlines or actions that need to be done.

- **Safari.** Access the iPad's built-in web browser.

- **Settings.** Configure your iPad and apps; this is where the magic happens.

- **Videos.** Press this button to access any videos that are stored on your iPad.

Notifications and the Control Center

You can also access information and settings on your iPad without actually opening the Settings app. If you swipe down from the top of the screen, the **Notifications** pane will appear (see Figure 1.2). Here's where you can see your schedule and any notifications you may have received from apps (news, weather, text messages, etc.). Press the **Today** button at the top to see your schedule for the day, as well as the weather forecast. If you have any notifications (go to **Settings > Notification Center** to enable notifications for individual apps), they will appear here too. Press the **All** button to see all your current notifications. To get rid of a notification, press the **X** to the right of the app, which will clear out that notification.

Figure 1.2 Notifications Pane

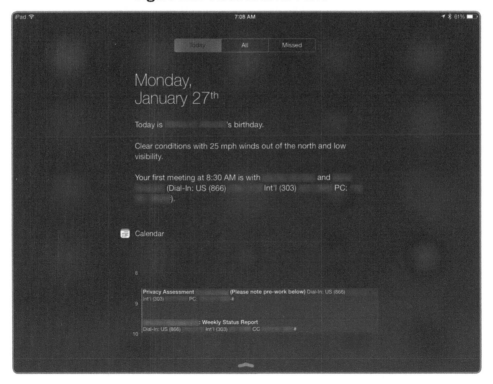

A simple swipe *up* from the bottom of your screen brings you the **Control Center** (see Figure 1.3), which is a great time-saver. It contains the settings you are likely to use most often, and you can access them much faster here than by going into the **Settings** app. From the Control Center you can do the following:

- enable or disable Airplane Mode
- turn Wi-Fi on or off
- turn Bluetooth on or off
- turn Do Not Disturb on or off
- turn the Screen Orientation Lock on or off
- go to your Timer
- go to your Camera
- play music, podcasts, or other audio with the mini-player
- adjust the iPad's volume
- adjust the iPad's brightness
- turn on and configure AirDrop
- turn on and configure AirPlay

Figure 1.3 Control Center

Browsing the Web

To get onto the web, just press the **Safari** button (icon) on your Home screen. The first time you do this, you'll see a blank window, ready for your instructions. Tap the **address bar** at the top of the window, and the iPad keyboard will pop up. Enter the URL of the site you want to visit, or put in a few search terms if you don't know exactly where to go. Google is your default search engine; you can change it by going to **Settings > Safari > Search Engine** and selecting either Google, Yahoo!, or Bing.

Safari acts mostly like the browser on your computer, but with fewer buttons (see Figure 1.4).

Figure 1.4 Safari

- The left- and right-facing arrows send you **Back** or **Forward**, so you can move back to the previous web page or forward to a new web page. But you don't have to use these buttons to move backward and forward; you can simply swipe right to return to a previously viewed page and then swipe left to go back to where you were before.

- Next to the arrows is a **Share** button, giving you a wide range of options:
  - use the AirDrop feature to share a web page instantly with other iPad or iPhone users near you (more on AirDrop in "Beyond the Lessons")
  - share via a message, email, or post to Twitter or Facebook
  - bookmark the web page or add it to your Reading List

- ○ add the page to your Home screen for easy access later
  - ○ copy or print the web page

- On the right side of the address bar is the **Bookmarks** button, which brings up a list of saved websites, favorites, your complete browsing history, and any pages saved to your Reading List. If you're a Twitter user, connect your account (via the **Twitter** page in **Settings**), and your Twitter feed will appear when you press the @ button.

- The next button, which looks like a cloud, will display your open iCloud tabs, if you have any. With iCloud, you can sync browser tabs between computers. Then you can use your iPad to view open tabs on other computers.

- The plus sign at the end allows you to create new tabs in the browser. You can also press down and hold the plus sign to see a list of **Recently Closed Tabs**.

- Within the address bar, you'll see either an **X** or a **circular arrow**. Click on the X to interrupt the download of a web page, or click the circular arrow to refresh the page you're already viewing.

When you first open a web page, you see the whole page, not just part of it. To get a closer look at the page, you need to use your fingers to zoom in. There are three ways to do this: (1) rotate your screen from Portrait to Landscape mode (if you were in Portrait mode to begin with); (2) do the "two-finger spread" (put your thumb and forefinger close together on the screen and move them apart); or (3) simply tap twice. Learn more about these shortcuts in "Beyond the Lessons."

Tip: If you want to read an article or story without all of a web page's annoying ads or links, just press the Reader button ≡ , and you'll get a clean, uncluttered page with just the text you want to read (more on reading apps in Lesson 5).

Once you have browsed a few web pages, you may be ready to save some of them as bookmarks. Tap the Share button ⬆ and press **Bookmark**. When you do, the following will appear (see Figure 1.5):

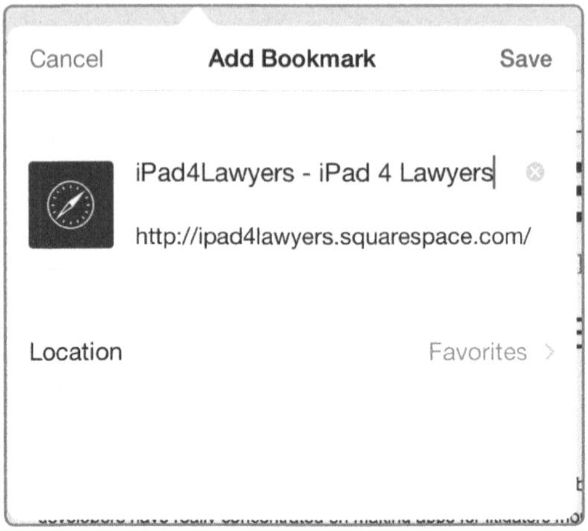

You can customize the name of your bookmark here, and by pressing the **Bookmarks** button you can specify where you want the bookmark to go—into the Bookmarks list or into a folder you create yourself (to create a folder, press the **Bookmarks** button, press **Edit**, and then press the **New Folder** button). Click **Done** on your keyboard, and you're done.

Figure 1.5 Bookmarking a Page

Cancel	**Add Bookmark**	Save
	iPad4Lawyers - iPad 4 Lawyers ⊗	
	http://ipad4lawyers.squarespace.com/	
Location		Favorites ›

To manage your bookmarks, tap on the **Bookmarks** button and then press **Edit**. You can do a few things here:

- Press **New Folder** to create a topical folder to better manage your bookmarks.
- Tap on ⊖ to delete a bookmark.
- Tap on the bookmark itself to edit the name or URL of the bookmark.
- Tap and hold on the lines ☰ to move the bookmark up or down to another location in the Bookmarks list.

That's it! Now you can start surfing the web and bookmark any sites you want to visit later.

Safari offers tabbed browsing, so you can keep multiple sites open by opening a new tab for each site. To open a new tab, just press the **plus sign** at the far top right. To delete a tab, press the **X** on the tab you want to remove. If you are using iCloud and sync your tabs from other computers, you can access tabs open on other computers or devices by pressing the **iCloud Tabs** button.

Tip: Want to browse the web without anyone tracking your every move? Just enable private browsing. Press the plus sign to bring up a new tab, and at the bottom left, press the **Private** button. You'll be asked whether you want to close or keep your existing tabs, and then you can browse privately to the site(s) of your choice.

Surfing the web on the iPad is a lot of fun and more satisfying than trying to view a website on a small smartphone. But the iPad offers so much more; let's get your email, calendars, and contacts set up next.

Setting Up Mail, Calendar, and Contacts

The lifeblood of a lawyer's practice arguably can be found in three types of digital data: email, calendar, and contacts. You'll want to be able to access this data as soon as you begin using your iPad, and in this lesson I'll show you how to do just that.

Figure 2.1 Settings Options

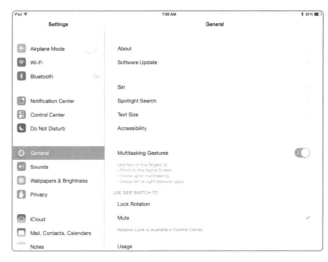

You configure your mail, calendar, and contacts through **Settings**, which is on the Home screen. Just press Settings and you'll see a wide range of options (see Figure 2.1).

Here you can configure most of the features of your iPad—Wi-Fi, how you receive notifications, security options, your wallpaper, and specific settings for many of the apps on your device.

For purposes of this lesson, we'll focus on the Mail, Contacts, Calendars settings, so click that now (see Figure 2.2).

Figure 2.2. Mail, Contacts, Calendars

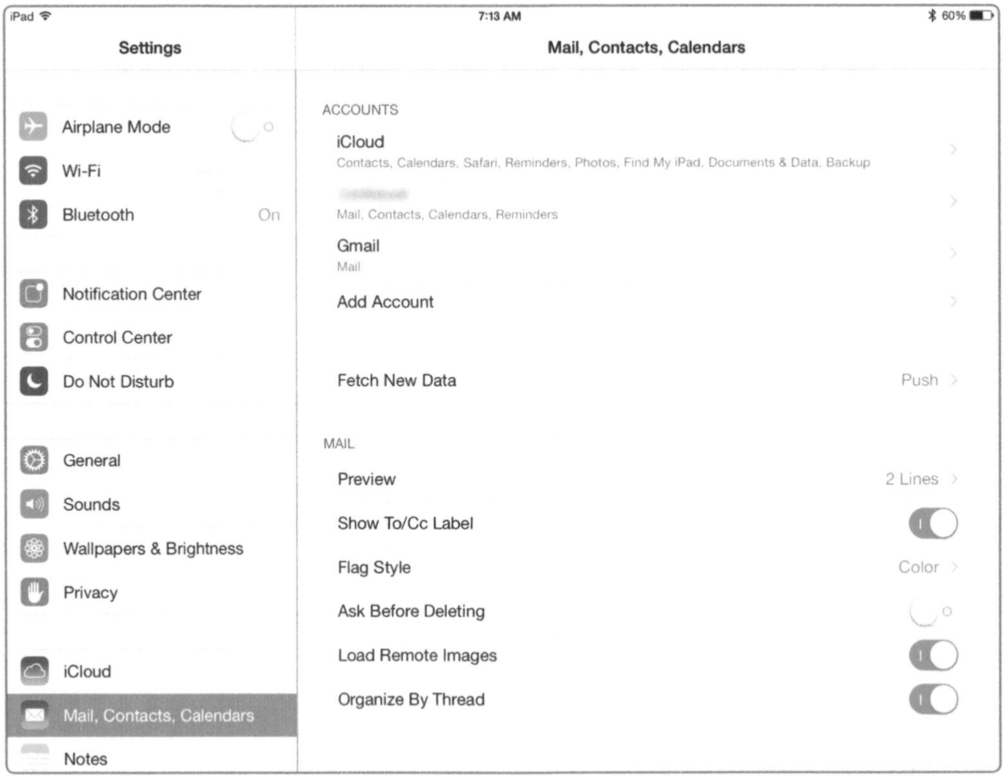

Then tap **Add Account**.

On the next screen, you'll see a menu of the different types of email accounts you can add:

- iCloud
- Microsoft Exchange
- Gmail

- Yahoo!
- AOL
- Outlook.com
- Other

Here's how to set up the most popular email services.

Microsoft Exchange

If you use Exchange to manage your mail, contacts, and calendars, it's very simple to connect your iPad to an existing account:

- Click on **Exchange**.
- Enter your email address.
- Enter the password on your account.
- Enter a description for the account, if you want.
- Press **Next**.
- If you get the message "Cannot Verify Server Identity," press **Continue**.
- If you get the message "Unable to Verify Certificate," press **Accept**.
- A field labeled **Server** will appear below Email—enter your Exchange server information.
- Enter your domain (this is optional; if you don't have one, don't worry).
- Enter your username (usually your email address).
- Press **Next**.
- If you get the message "Unable to Verify Certificate" again, don't worry—just press **Accept**.

The iPad asks what information you want to synchronize between your iPad and Exchange: **Mail, Contacts, Calendar, Notes**. If you select

Calendar or Contacts, you'll receive a message asking whether you want to keep or delete the local data on your device. Because this is likely the first time you have synced your iPad, there probably isn't any local data. So select either **Keep** to preserve your existing contacts or calendar items or **Delete** to get rid of any contacts or calendar items that currently exist on your device.

Press **Save**, and your device can now accept mail, contacts, and calendar items from your Exchange server.

iCloud

iCloud is not exactly email; it's a service that allows you to sync your mail, contacts, and calendar (among other things) across all of your devices, whether you have a Mac, PC, iPhone, or iPad. If you already have an iCloud account, just enter your Apple login information. If you set up your iPad in iTunes (see "Getting Started"), use that username and password. If you don't have an Apple login, just press the **Get a Free Apple ID** button. Once you fill out the requested information, you'll get an iCloud account with 5 GB of free storage (you can upgrade to more space for a fee).

The screen that follows your login allows you to select the items you want to sync. You can choose to sync the following items:

- Mail
- Contacts
- Calendars
- Reminders
- Safari Bookmarks
- Notes
- Keychain (saves and synchronizes all your passwords)
- Photos

- Documents and Data (allows any app on your iPad that creates documents or other data to store them in iCloud)
- Find My iPad

Select the items you want to sync, and press **Save**. You can adjust these settings at any time by choosing iCloud in **Settings**.

Gmail, Yahoo!, and Outlook.com

If you have one or more Gmail, Yahoo!, or Outlook.com accounts, the configuration options are identical. Here's how to access these webmail services on the iPad:

- Enter your name.
- Enter your Gmail, Yahoo!, or Outlook.com email address.
- Enter your password.
- Enter a description, if you want.
- Press **Next**.
- On the next screen, select whether you want to sync Mail, Calendars, or Notes.
- Press **Save**.

If you don't see your email provider listed, all is not lost—just press **Other**, **Add Mail Account**, and follow the directions for setting up the email account. (See "Beyond the Lessons" for instructions on setting up other email types, as well as setting up your email, calendars, and contacts from within iTunes.)

The Rest of the Options

Now that you've set up your email account(s), you have some more decisions to make. The **Mail, Contacts, Calendars** area has quite a few settings to configure; for example, the number of messages to show, creating and using a signature for email, and the minimum font size. Explanations for these settings is in "Beyond the Lessons" under **Advanced Email Options**; be sure to read about these settings once you have more time to play with your iPad.

Using the Universal Inbox

One of the most convenient features of the iPad (depending on how you like to use email, that is) is the Universal Inbox. When you go to the Mail app in Landscape mode, you can see a list of all your email accounts in the left pane—if you can't see the list, press the **Mailboxes** button in the upper left corner. At the top of the list is an option for **All Inboxes**, also known as the Universal Inbox. If you choose this option, you'll see email from all the accounts you've configured on your iPad merged into one list and displayed in chronological order from newest to oldest.

If you want to view email from only one account, you'll find inboxes for each of your accounts just below your Universal Inbox. Press on that account's inbox to see only the email sent to that account. To dig more deeply into a particular email account (for example, to see folders that you have set up to store email messages), go to the **Accounts** section and choose the account you want to view.

You will also see that there are separate mailboxes for **VIP** and **Flagged** messages. Use the VIP mailbox to filter messages from "important" people—just select VIP on the Mailboxes list and press **Add VIP** to add VIP senders from your Contacts. If you like to flag your messages so you can come back later and act on them, press the **Flag** button above the email message when you are reading it. Then you can go to the **Flagged** folder to see all the flagged messages in one place.

You can also add favorite folders from your email accounts to the Mailboxes list. Let's say you have an important client that you want to monitor with its own mailbox. Just tap **Edit** while in the Mailboxes list and then **Add Mailbox**. Browse through your individual email folders and select the ones you want to make favorites. Once selected, they will appear as separate "mailboxes" on your primary Mailboxes list.

Now that your email, calendars, and contacts are all set up, you're ready to learn more about navigating your iPad and organizing the apps you have.

Managing Your iPad: Multitasking and Folders

Now that you've got your iPad up and running and your mail, calendar, and contacts are all set, it's time to start getting organized. In this lesson, we'll talk about multitasking on your iPad and how to organize your apps into folders.

Multitasking

One of the unfortunate limitations of the iPad when it was first released was that you couldn't work with different applications without first closing one and opening another. This anti-multitasking approach that Apple initially took had a simple enough explanation: working within a single app allows a person to be more focused, efficient, and productive. Besides, multitasking is for geeks, right?

Users soon found serious drawbacks to the approach. They couldn't listen to music from apps like Spotify or Pandora and work in other apps at the same time. When they wanted to check email in the middle of an instant messaging (IM) conversation, they had to quit the IM program, check email, and then wait for the IM program to start up again.

Apple finally saw the light, and today's iPad allows multitasking, although it's probably not what you're used to on your personal computer. Still, moving between programs on your iPad is pretty simple—here's how:

- When you're working in one app and need to move to another recently opened app, either (1) press the **Home** button twice or (2) swipe up with a four- or five-finger swipe.

- The application you're working in will move up, exposing a smaller screenshot of that app and the app icon beneath it. You can swipe to the left to scroll through all of your other open apps.

- If you change your mind and decide to go back to the app you were using, just (1) press the **Home** button twice or (2) swipe down with a four- or five-finger swipe, and you will be back in the original app.

- To go to another recently opened application, just tap on the image of the app or the app icon below.

- If you can't see the app you want on the task bar, just swipe to the left, and you'll see all your recently opened apps.

When you're not using these open apps, they exist in "suspended" mode; when you revisit one, it will pick up where you left off the last time you used it. However, with the release of iOS 7, some apps will "refresh" when you return to them. There will be a short delay, which can be annoying.

When you open an app, it won't close by itself; it remains "open" until you close it. Over time, you might find your task bar filling up with dozens of apps you never closed. To quit an app, simply swipe up on the screenshot, and it will disappear from the list of open apps.

Folders

As you accumulate apps, you'll find they begin to spread over more and more screens. When you install an app, the iPad simply adds it to the next available spot and keeps on going, without any rhyme or reason. Unfortunately, there *is* a limit; currently iPad users are limited to fifteen screens. With twenty apps per screen, plus the six apps along the bottom of the screen, the maximum number of apps is 306.

Some of you may never come close to having 300 apps on your iPad, but I'll bet that some of you might—after all, with so many great free apps out there, it's easy to get carried away. Even if you don't install hundreds of apps, having multiple screens to page through and search for your apps can be a real hassle. You can always use the Search function to look for a particular app (to access **Search**, simply drag your finger down on any screen, and Spotlight Search will appear at the top of the screen). But wouldn't it be great if there were a better way to organize all of those apps?

Fortunately, there is, and it's ridiculously simple. The iPad allows you to create folders on your device, and each folder can hold up to 135 apps. Here's how to do it:

- Press down and hold an app you want to move into a folder until it (and the other apps) start to jiggle.
- Move the app's icon on top of another app that you want to include in the same folder.
- A folder will be created instantly, and when you release the icon you're moving, the folder will contain those two apps.
- Your iPad will automatically name the folder based on the content of the apps. If you like the name, just press the **Home** button, and your folder is complete. If you want to change the name of the folder, just type in the space listing the current name and edit the title. Then press the **Home** button to finish.

- Adding other apps to a folder is easy—while the apps are in "jiggle" mode, just tap and hold one of them, and drag it over the folder you've created.

- If the app you're moving into a folder is on a different screen from the folder itself, just drag the app icon left or right, depending on where the folder is located, and go from screen to screen until you reach the screen with the desired folder.

You can set up folders for news, entertainment, games, travel, productivity, law, and any other category you like. To access the apps in a folder, press on that folder—it will unfold and display the first screen of the apps in it. If you have more than nine apps in the folder, you'll have to swipe to the left to see the rest. Suddenly the number of apps you can keep on your iPad has expanded exponentially. Let's do the math: 20 folders per page times 135 apps per folder times 15 possible pages equals an incredible 40,500 apps—oops, make that 40,506 if you include the apps at the bottom of the screen. This is only theoretical, because your iPad probably doesn't have enough space on it to hold that many. The point is, you can store many more apps on your iPad, and it makes sense to organize them using folders.

Searching on Your iPad

The iPad's **Spotlight Search** is a marvelous tool—you can search for *anything* with it. Anything on your iPad, that is: apps, contacts, email, documents. If it's on your iPad, Spotlight Search can find it. But do you really need all that power? It may be that your search results are *too* long—but don't worry, there's a way to fix this. You can configure Spotlight to search only those applications you want. To do this, go to **Settings > General > Spotlight Search**. There you'll see a list of all the things included in a search. Press on those items you don't want, and they will be excluded from your next search.

Managing Apps in iTunes

You might find that moving around your apps on the iPad is time-consuming and inefficient. There's another way to manage and organize your apps using iTunes, and it's relatively simple, especially if you're more comfortable using a mouse to move things around. Here's how to do it.

Connect your iPad to your computer and open iTunes. Look for **Devices** and click on **iPad**. When you see the iPad's main screen in iTunes, look for **Apps** at the top of the screen and click it. You'll see two views: (1) a list of all of your apps on the left and (2) screenshots of all your iPad screens on the right (see Figure 3.1).

Figure 3.1 iPad Apps and Screenshots Shown in iTunes

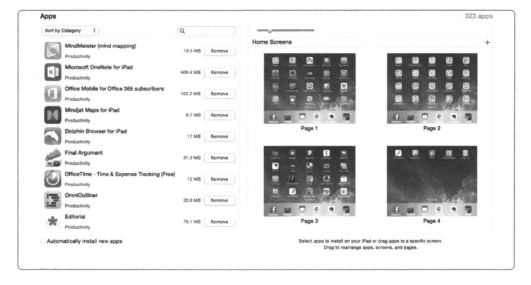

Organizing. To move apps from screen to screen using iTunes, just select the app you want to move by clicking on the screenshot and dragging it down to the screen of your choice. The view at the top will change to that screen, and you will then be able to place the app icon anywhere on that screen. To move the app into a folder, simply hold the app over the desired folder; the folder will open, and you can place the app icon anywhere you choose within the folder.

Deleting. If you no longer want an app on your iPad, there are a couple of ways to delete it. *Caution*: When you delete an app from your iPad, you also delete all the documents or other data you created with it. If you want to keep application data, see Lesson 4 before you delete the app. Here's how to delete an app:

- On your iPad, press and hold the app's icon until it begins to jiggle; a black **X** will appear in the upper left corner. Press the X, and you'll be asked to confirm the deletion.

- Within iTunes, scroll down the list of apps on the left side of the **Apps** page, and uncheck the app(s) you want removed from the iPad. The next time you sync the iPad with your computer, the app will be removed from the device.

Note: Neither of these options actually deletes the app from your computer—to do that, you'll need to click on the **Apps** link under **Library** in iTunes. From there, just right-click on any app and select **Delete**, and you'll have the option of removing it completely from your computer.

Now that you've got your apps organized, it's time to add some content. Let's start moving files onto your iPad.

Adding Files to Your iPad and Syncing Them

As much as I love the iPad, even I must admit that one of its biggest drawbacks is how it stores files. Unlike PCs or Macs, the iPad has no document folders, so there's no direct way to store or organize your documents, spreadsheets, presentations, images, videos, or any other kind of files. Instead, you must access those files through individual apps. Further, physically transferring files to your tablet has its challenges; the iPad has no USB port to which a computer or hard drive could be connected, nor does it have an SD card slot to provide additional storage.

But don't lose heart—there are several ways to transfer files to your iPad, and in this lesson we will discuss two of them: (1) file sharing in iTunes and (2) using cloud-based apps to access your files.

Sharing Files between Your iPad and a Computer

Transferring files between your iPad and a computer is actually very easy, although it's not terribly intuitive. Because the iPad syncs with iTunes, you must use iTunes to transfer files between the device and your computer. Another caveat is that you will only be able to transfer files from apps that support File Sharing. Fortunately, more and more apps are supporting File Sharing, especially those that handle documents and files. However, files can only be opened by apps that support the particular file type; so before transferring a file as described below, make sure you know which file types each of your iPad apps supports.

Here's how to copy files to your iPad using File Sharing:

- Connect the iPad to your computer.
- Launch iTunes on your computer (you must be using iTunes 9.1 or later to take advantage of File Sharing).
- Once iTunes connects, go to the **Devices** section and select **iPad**.
- Click the **Apps** button from the choices across the top of the screen to see all of the apps currently installed on your iPad.
- Scroll down below the apps to the section marked **File Sharing** (see Figure 4.1). There you will see a list of all the applications that support File Sharing. If you do not see the File Sharing section, that means you don't currently have any apps that support the function.

Figure 4.1 File Sharing

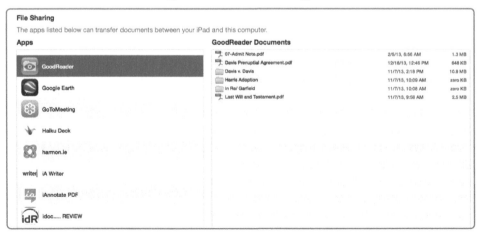

- Click on an application. To the right, you'll see a list of all the documents currently stored in that application.

At this point, you have a couple of options, depending on whether you want to transfer documents to or from the iPad.

- Here's how to move documents *to* your iPad *from* the computer:
  - Make sure you have selected the correct app under File Sharing.
  - Click the **Add** button; a dialog box will appear, allowing you to navigate to the documents you want to add. Again, make sure you select only files supported by that particular app. Click the **Open** button in the dialog box, and the selected files will be added.
  - Alternatively, you can open a document folder on your computer and drag and drop the documents directly from the folder into the File Sharing section in iTunes.

- Here's how to move documents *from* your iPad *to* the computer:
  - Make sure you have selected the correct app under File Sharing.
  - Highlight the files you want to move, and then click the **Save to** button.
  - Locate the folder on your computer to which you want to move the files, and click **Choose** to save the files.
  - If the destination folder on your computer is already open, you can just drag and drop the files into that folder.

Using AirDrop to Share Files and Other Things

Apple calls its latest sharing feature AirDrop, and it's a seriously cool way to share things with others who also have iPads or iPhones. AirDrop will transfer files between nearby Apple devices wirelessly and with only a few taps of a button. Here's how to use it:

- First, AirDrop must be enabled on both the sending and receiving devices. Swipe up from the bottom of the screen to show the **Control Panel**, and press the **AirDrop** button. Select **Everyone**, or choose **Contacts Only** if you just want to share a file with people in your Contacts list.

- Open the app containing the file you want to share, and select it. Press the **Share** button ⬆. The first option will be **AirDrop** (see Figure 4.2). Press it.

- If the receiving device has AirDrop turned on, you will see that person's icon pop up on your app. Press the icon to get the process started.

- If you have the receiving device, the message "[Name] would like to share [file, website, etc.]" will appear. Press **Accept** to receive it or **Decline** to reject it.

- If you press **Accept**, a list of apps will appear. Select the app you want to view the file in, and the transferred file will appear in that app.

Figure 4.2 AirDrop

A Better Way to Access Files: Cloud-Based Services

If using iTunes to transfer files is a hassle for you, there's an easier, more convenient, and in many ways better method to transfer and access files on your iPad. By taking advantage of apps that store your files in the cloud, you can wirelessly transfer documents and other files directly to your iPad.

You have probably heard of cloud computing by now—it refers to apps and services that store your data on other computers (popularly known as the cloud). These services give you access to your data from any device with an Internet connection. If you use web-based email like Gmail or Yahoo!, you're using a cloud-computing service. As a wireless device, the iPad is particularly suited to working with cloud-computing services.

The following are some of the most popular cloud-based services you can use to store files and access them on your iPad.

The first is **Dropbox** (http://db.tt/JCp3V5J), an easy-to-use service that allows you to sync your files online and across all of your computers. Dropbox is a logical first choice because it is built into just about any app worth having on the iPad, and its ubiquity makes it very convenient to use. To get started with Dropbox, you'll first need to download the application to your computer; there are versions for Windows, Mac, and Linux platforms. Once it's installed (you'll be prompted to create an account), Dropbox simply creates a new folder on your computer: My Dropbox. Just drag files and folders into the My Dropbox folder, and Dropbox will sync them automatically to your online account.

After you've installed Dropbox on one computer, install it on another computer that you use. Now you can access all of your Dropbox files, no matter which computer you're using. Dropbox also allows you to share folders or individual files with other people so you can work on documents together or provide access to files for others to view. A free Dropbox account provides 2 GB of online storage. Paid accounts provide up to 500 GB for individuals and 1 TB or more for teams (monthly rates vary).

Now that you've got Dropbox on your computer(s), it's time to install it on your iPad (Dropbox is also available on the iPhone, BlackBerry, and Android). Go to the App Store and search for Dropbox; the download is free. Once you've entered your Dropbox login information, you'll have access to your entire My Dropbox folder—and all of your files and documents—right there on your iPad (see Figure 4.3).

Figure 4.3 My Dropbox on the iPad

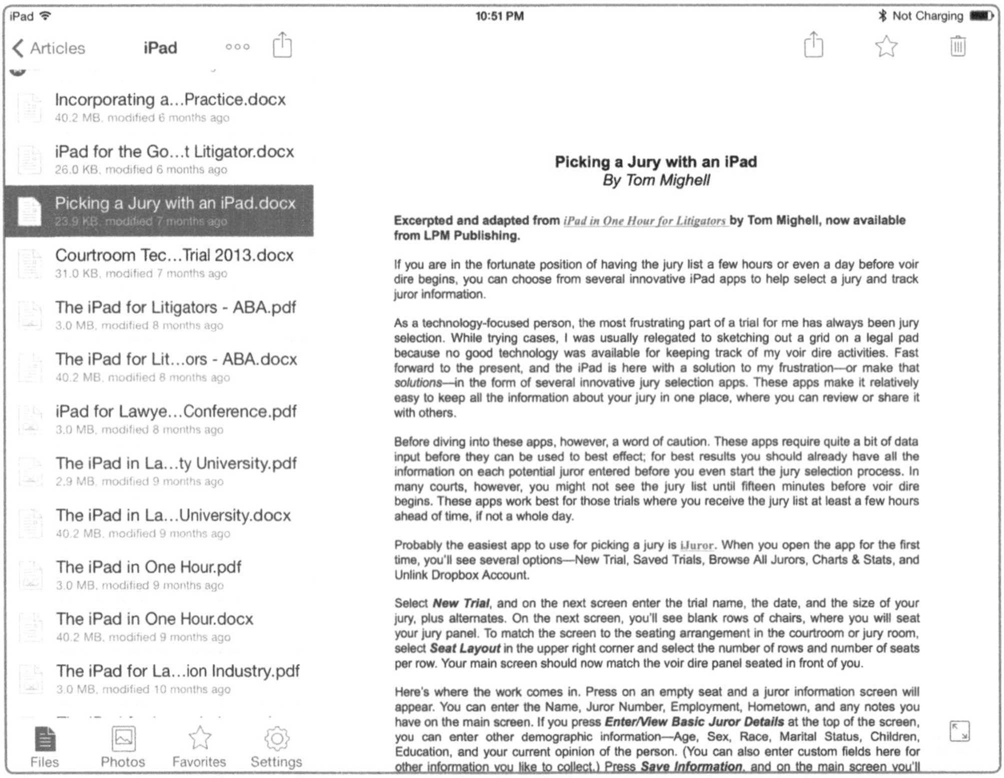

Simply select a file to view it. Dropbox will let you view just about any file type, whether it's a spreadsheet, PDF, presentation, or image. If you want to edit a document in Dropbox, there's bad news and good news. The bad news is that editing is not available in the app—it is pretty much just a document viewer. The good news is that there are a number of apps that work directly with Dropbox to help you edit your documents. One such app is Documents To Go; you can use the app to open a Word or Excel document stored on Dropbox, make your edits, and have those edits saved back to your Dropbox folder. I'll talk more about Documents To Go in Lesson 5.

Other reputable services offering features similar to Dropbox are **Box** (www.box.com) and **SpiderOak** (www.spideroak.com). They also have comparable iPad apps, which allow you to access all of your desktop or laptop files on your iPad. No matter which option you choose, spend some time on the website of any file-management service before making a final decision about which one is best for you.

One of the advantages to using a service like Dropbox is that you don't even need to install the Dropbox app on your iPad to access your files. So many apps directly integrate with Dropbox that it is simple to get to your Dropbox files from your device. Of the other cloud services, Box is integrated into a good number of apps, with SpiderOak and others pulling up the rear.

Many iPad apps connect with other apps (like Dropbox and Documents To Go); these connections are how the iPad compensates for not having a folder system. If an app communicates with other apps, you'll see the ⬆ button somewhere on the screen. Press it, and you'll see a list of all the apps that will open the file you have selected.

If you prefer direct access to your laptop or desktop files, try a remote access app like **Splashtop 2 Remote Desktop** (http://bit.ly/1iqjE3T) or **Jump Desktop** (http://bit.ly/18fIWI8). These apps provide a connection from your iPad to your computer, where you can work directly with the files located there. You'll need to install the software on your laptop or desktop before you can access your files remotely (the apps include basic instructions on how to do this), but this method is a secure way to get to your files.

Security and Cloud-Based File Management

When I talk to lawyers about the iPad and mention Dropbox, I am invariably asked, "Is Dropbox secure?" The short answer is *yes*, but with some qualifications. Unlike many other cloud-based file-management services, Dropbox provides only a single encryption key for your data, for use both by you as well as Dropbox Support, in case you need assistance. By contrast, other companies provide you with your own encryption key, so you retain ultimate control over your data. Dropbox states that it has very strict controls that prohibit employee access to user data, and the chances that a Dropbox employee would access your information are likely extremely small. Further, in 2013, the Electronic Frontier Foundation found that Dropbox (and SpiderOak as well) implemented five out of five best practices for encryption in the Who Has Your Back? program.

No matter which cloud service you use to manage your files, the security of confidential information should be of paramount importance. If you want to install Dropbox but you're still worried about its security, use a tool like **Viivo** (www.viivo.com) or **Boxcryptor** (www.boxcryptor.com) to provide an extra layer of security. These products create a fully encrypted folder *within* your Dropbox folder, so only you have access to the data. Another option is to use an Internet-connected hard drive like the **Transporter** (www.filetransporter.com). Once you connect the Transporter to the Internet, you can synchronize files between all of your computers, without the need to store documents with a service like Dropbox.

In the end, if the security issue is just too much for you, you can always use Dropbox for your non-confidential files and load confidential files onto your iPad by emailing them to yourself or using the File Sharing feature in iTunes. These alternatives are not the most convenient or efficient, but they offer the most security.

Other-File Management Tips

Backing up your files. You should regularly back up your iPad to make sure the data on it is always protected. There are a couple of ways to do this. The first, and most complete, is to sync your iPad with iTunes. To sync with a cabled connection, plug the iPad into your computer, fire up iTunes, and press the **Sync** button. However, you can also perform a wireless sync without physically connecting to iTunes. Here's how to set it up:

- Connect your iPad and the computer with **iTunes** to the same wireless network.
- Connect your iPad to that computer and launch iTunes (if it doesn't automatically launch).
- Highlight **iPad** in the left-hand menu.
- Click **Summary** in the menu bar at the top of the screen and scroll down to the **Options** section.
- Check the box next to **Sync with this iPad over Wi-Fi**. Click **Apply**.
- Disconnect your iPad from the computer.
- To sync, go to **Settings** > **General** > **iTunes Wi-Fi Sync** > **Sync Now**. Your iPad will automatically sync with iTunes on your computer—no wires involved!

Unfortunately, if you lose a file, you cannot selectively restore it from an iTunes backup; you will have to completely restore your iPad to get that file back. So it's a good idea to frequently back up the files you have created on your iPad to a folder on your computer; that's why using online services like Dropbox provides an extra level of confidence.

Deleting apps. If you delete an app from your iPad, you also delete all the files on the iPad associated with the app. That's why backing up your shared files is so important, especially before you delete the app from the iPad—see above.

Removing files from your iPad. If you have a file you no longer need, there are two ways to delete it from your iPad:

- First, determine whether the app itself allows you to delete files. In most apps you can find this out simply by swiping the particular file to the left—a red **DELETE** button will appear if the app supports deletion. Just press that button to delete the file.
- If the app in question does not support deletion (this is now rare—most apps support deletion of files), you'll need to remove the file from within iTunes:
  - Connect the iPad to your computer and start **iTunes**.
  - Go to **Devices** (on the left) and select **iPad**; click on the **Apps** tab.
  - Scroll down to the **File Sharing** section, and select the application from which you want to delete the file.
  - From the files that appear in the **Documents** list to the right, highlight the file you want to delete.
  - Press the **Delete** key on your keyboard. You'll be prompted on-screen to confirm the deletion.
  - The file is deleted immediately from your iPad.

You have learned to move files onto your iPad and organize them. Now let's take a look at some of the apps that can help you create documents in your practice.

Being Productive on the iPad

Now that you've completed the first four lessons, your iPad should be set up and ready to use. You've configured your email, calendar, and contacts; learned how to multitask and organize your apps into folders; and mastered the art of transferring files between your iPad and computer. Now it's time to learn how to really *use* the iPad in your work or law practice.

Some claim Apple designed the iPad only for content *consumption* and that it makes a poor content *creation* device. Indeed, there are thousands of fantastic apps that allow you to read books, magazines, and news; watch television, movies, or other video content; connect with your friends on social networking sites; educate school kids about different subjects; and play games. These apps just feel right on the iPad.

However, over the past four years, as people discovered more and more ways to put the iPad to work, we have seen an explosion in the number of apps designed to create content, including apps that help you shoot, edit, and manage photos and videos; write and publish music; and write and publish blog posts, documents, and books. At first glance, using a tablet for drafting documents—arguably a lawyer's prime activity—may seem a bit awkward. Lawyers may not feel comfortable using the on-screen keyboard to tap out notes or write a letter to a client. The lack of a physical keyboard is one reason many legal professionals remain skeptical about using the iPad as a tool for practicing law.

In this lesson, I'll try to dispel the reluctance about using the iPad to create content and look directly at some ways lawyers are using the device to create notes, documents, spreadsheets, and even presentations. I'll also share some of my favorite ways that lawyers can conduct meetings, brainstorm, and review legal research, all on the iPad.

Before you start. One of the reasons it's hard to think of the iPad as a content creation device is that getting content into the thing can be a challenge. True enough—in Lesson 4 we discussed a few ways to move documents and other files onto your iPad. Fortunately, when it comes to taking notes and creating documents, you're not limited to the on-screen keyboard. Let's look at a few tools that can help level the playing field when it comes to content creation. Because we only have an hour together in this book, I'll mention just a few of my favorites and leave it to you to explore the other options.

Keyboard. A keyboard, you ask? Surely not. The whole point of a tablet computer is to do away with the keyboard. And you'd be right—mostly. But if you're truly interested in using the iPad for content creation, and even potentially as a laptop replacement, you *must* have a physical keyboard. A number of terrific options are available.

The first is from Apple. The **Apple Wireless Keyboard** (http://bit.ly/ 9jTTxM) connects to your iPad using Bluetooth; here's how to "pair" the keyboard (or any other Bluetooth device) with your tablet:

- Make sure the keyboard is turned on (the wireless keyboard is battery powered).
- On the iPad, go to **Settings** > **General** > **Bluetooth**.
- Make sure the **Bluetooth** option is turned **ON**. When it is, your iPad will begin searching for Bluetooth-enabled devices and list them under **Devices**. Your keyboard should be listed there (see Figure 5.1). Press on it to connect.

Figure 5.1 Connecting Keyboard Using Bluetooth

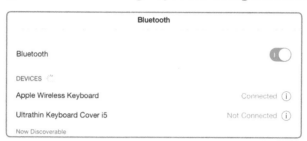

- A message from the iPad will prompt you to type a series of numbers. Use the keyboard to type those numbers and press **Enter**.
- Your wireless keyboard is now paired with the iPad, and you can begin to use it immediately.

In my opinion, the Apple Wireless Keyboard is the best option because it is a full-size keyboard. If you want something a little bit more compact, my recommendation at this time is the **Logitech Ultrathin Keyboard Cover** (http://bit.ly/1c1Ejm3). It serves both as a keyboard and as a cover for your iPad when you are not using it. There's a magnetic slot just above the keyboard that holds the tablet when you are typing (see Figure 5.2). When you're done, just align the keyboard with the strong hinge magnet, and your iPad screen is now protected by the keyboard.

For other keyboard suggestions, visit **iLounge** (www.ilounge.com) for product reviews and more.

Figure 5.2 Logitech Ultrathin Keyboard Cover

Stand. With the advent of Apple's **Smart Cover** (http://bit.ly/199vg1s) and other covers that double as stands, you may not need a separate stand upon which to prop your iPad. However, many people prefer to use a stand as an easel or as something to hold the iPad when it's not in use. There are dozens of stands reviewed at iLounge; among the best rated is one of my favorites, the Twelve South **Compass** (http://twelvesouth.com/products/compass/) portable stand. It looks a bit like an easel, allowing you to display the iPad in either Portrait or Landscape mode and type away with your wireless keyboard. There's also a foldaway secondary leg that can be used to create a workstation angled just right for typing on the on-screen keyboard (if you want to do that). The best part about the Compass is its size; it can accommodate either an iPad Air or iPad Mini, and when folded, it's 7 inches long by 1 inch wide, making it easy to store and transport. A word of caution, however: on an X-ray the Compass can look a little like a sharp object, so when you're traveling through airport security, you will probably want to take it out of your bag and put it in a security bin.

Stylus. No doubt many of you, like me, purchased the iPad with the intent of using it as a true tablet device—that is, to use it like a legal pad to take notes at meetings, depositions, and the like. Unfortunately, my handwriting is not the best, so I don't use a stylus very often. But if you are comfortable with writing, you'll probably want to take advantage of the iPad's ability to capture written notes. And finding the right stylus is the first place to start.

Like stands and cases, there are a *lot* of different styli available for the iPad. One thing they all have in common is an iPad-compatible tip. An iPad's touchscreen won't respond to a hard, pointy stylus. Go ahead, try to write on the screen with a hard, pointy object (but don't try too hard or you'll damage the screen!)—it just won't work.

That's because the iPad has what is known as a capacitive touchscreen; to write effectively on it, the tip of the stylus must mimic how your fingertip conducts electricity when you touch the screen. My current favorite stylus is the **Wacom Bamboo** (http://bit.ly/1eygJjO)—the tip is relatively small and the weight of the stylus comes close to that of a real pen.

Recently, technologies that use the iPad's Bluetooth connection have made possible battery-powered styli that offer a lot more control and precision than the traditional rubber-tipped options. One of these is the new **Adonit Jot Script** (http://bit.ly/182ubvu), which has a tip that looks very much like a ballpoint pen. Although it works best with apps that can connect to the stylus, the Jot Script should work in any app.

Of course, you can always write notes with your finger as well. Some of the apps mentioned below allow fingertip note taking, although you might want to use a stylus if you need more control over what you're writing.

Printer. Once you've taken your notes, you might want to print them. There are two ways to print from your iPad. First, you can use **AirPrint**, an iPad feature that allows you to print wirelessly to a compatible printer. If you don't have an AirPrint-enabled printer, you can use a printing app, which will print to any printer.

There are dozens of printers that are compatible with AirPrint, including models from Brother, Canon, Epson, Hewlett Packard, and Lexmark. A full list of printers with AirPrint functionality is on the "AirPrint Basics" page (http://support.apple.com/kb/ht4356) on Apple's website. If you have a compatible printer, press the **Print** or **Print File** button in your iPad app, and you'll see a box like Figure 5.3.

Figure 5.3 Printing from the iPad

Press **Select Printer** to choose the printer, and then tap to select the page range and number of copies. After you press **Print**, your printer should begin to print the file from your iPad.

Even if you don't have a printer that works with AirPrint, you can still print from your iPad using apps designed specifically for that purpose. Two good printing app options are **Printer Pro** (http://bit.ly/sdd2T1) and **FileCentral** (http://bit.ly/rDCVPN). These apps work by connecting to the printer through your computer, so you must connect your iPad and computer through the same wireless network. When you use one of these apps to print, the iPad sends a command through the computer directly to the printer, which then prints the document.

These apps can be a bit cumbersome to use—you first need to move the document you want to print into the printer app itself—and you cannot print directly from the application that creates or stores the document. But if you don't have an AirPrint-enabled printer, apps like these are your best bet.

Tip: If you don't have an AirPrint printer and don't want to use these apps, check out the **Lantronix xPrintServer** (http://bit.ly/Pr3poq)—it connects via USB or Wi-Fi to your printer(s), allowing you to print directly from your iPad. You can connect up to eight USB printers and an unlimited number of networked computers in your office.

Getting Started: Taking Notes

Before we graduate to full document preparation, let's start with the basics and take some notes. There are dozens of note-taking apps for the iPad, all with varying levels of features. They are intended primarily for you to take handwritten notes with a stylus (or your finger, but I suggest a stylus), but some of the apps also support text entry using the on-screen or stand-alone keyboard. Here are a few apps I recommend.

Noteshelf (http://bit.ly/1b6HPyS)

Features

- keep notes in notebooks on a virtual shelf
- customize notebooks with dozens of cover and paper types
- can import and annotate PDF files
- works with digital styli like Jot Script

Pros

- excellent writing surface—wrist protection is good, and zoom feature allows you to fit more text on a page
- extensive selection of ballpoint or fountain pens and pencils with hundreds of colors
- share to Dropbox or Evernote to get your notes off the iPad

Con

- fewer features overall than other apps like Note Taker HD

Note Taker HD (http://bit.ly/1j8sYHE)

Features

- organize pages into documents or folders
- make flowcharts and insert shapes, text boxes, borders, and more
- save notes as PDF files

Pros

- a huge feature set—lots of options and customizations
- very powerful: "staple" documents together, create duplicate pages or notebooks, flag documents by priority, and reorder pages in a notebook

Cons

- can't save PDF files to Dropbox, Evernote, or other services
- huge feature set is overwhelming—screen is busy and features are hard to find

Penultimate (http://bit.ly/InQTEP)

Features

- owned by Evernote, so tightly integrated; save notes directly into Evernote
- designed to work with Jot Script

Pros

- very easy to understand and use
- makes text notes searchable, so you can even search your handwriting

Cons

- features limited compared with other apps
- no zoom feature
- no keyboard text entry—only handwritten note taking

Notability (http://bit.ly/1bbVKzb)

Features

- records audio of meetings, conferences, or other gatherings while you take notes
- audio syncs with typewritten notes, so you can tap part of your notes and listen to the recording from that point

Pros

- audio recording ideal for clarifying confusing notes
- easy to insert images, web clips, figures, or text boxes
- can share in multiple formats (with audio recording included); send to email, Dropbox, Google Drive, Twitter, Box, iTunes, and more

Cons

- folder and note organization not as clean as in other apps
- audio playback works with typewritten notes but not handwriting

7notes HD Premium (http://bit.ly/1j8tkOG)

Features

- handwriting recognition—will turn your handwriting into text
- three modes of writing: handwriting, handwriting to text, and keyboard to text
- export document as a PDF or share via email, Twitter, Facebook, or Evernote

Pros

- good for those who don't want handwritten notes but would prefer to write rather than type
- suggests how to complete words you write; just press on a button to complete the word

Cons

- correcting mistakes in handwriting recognition can take longer than typing notes out in the first place
- good for short notes or emails but not long documents
- no sync to Dropbox

Editorial (http://bit.ly/Izf6Yr)

Features

- a basic but very powerful text editor, great for typing when you don't want distractions
- Markdown (formatting especially designed for conversion to HTML format) preview will show you the final output of your document, if you plan to create an HTML file
- automatically syncs your notes as text or Markdown files to your Dropbox account
- Advanced users can take advantage of unique workflows to do even more with text files

Pros

- does one thing very well: edits text
- Dropbox integration is key to managing notes

Cons

- cannot write with this app; must type notes
- can only export files in HTML or plain text
- limited formatting options

Outlining Apps. Instead of free-form handwriting or typing, some lawyers prefer the structure of an outline. You'll find a number of great outlining apps for the iPad; my favorites are **OmniOutliner 2** (http://bit.ly/1hcV9WO) and **Outliner** (http://bit.ly/1k4B3jl). Both apps are easy to use, have some great additional features, and will create nice outlines for your deposition, meeting, or presentation.

Document Creation on the iPad

Note-taking apps work great for meetings, interviews, depositions, or when listening to a trial or hearing testimony. But if you have to churn out legal documents, you need a serious word processor. And while the iPad features a number of great word processing applications, none of them, in my opinion anyway, are truly serious. After all, they're apps, not full-fledged programs. As a result, the features and functions of these apps are pretty limited when you compare them with Microsoft Word, Pages for Mac, or Corel WordPerfect. As of this writing we're still waiting for an "app-ified" version of Microsoft Office, but even when (or if) it does become available, don't expect it to provide all the functionality of the full version.

Nevertheless, you still want to have a word processing app on your iPad for those times when you need to create or simply edit a document, spreadsheet, or presentation. Here's a recommended list of iPad document-creation options and some things to think about before you try them. Most of these suites can create and edit documents, spreadsheets, and presentations, with varying degrees of success. **CloudOn** actually provides access to real versions of Word, Excel, and PowerPoint—but with some caveats.

iWork

Because the iPad is an Apple product, we'll start with Apple's productivity suite—it's likely to be the most integrated into the iPad's functionality. Further, if you buy a new iPad (starting with the iPad Air and Mini with

Retina Display), you'll be able to download the entire iWork suite free of charge.

Pages (http://bit.ly/1b8ZKEa) is Apple's word processing app, and although it provides only a basic set of features and functions compared with the full-powered Mac version, it's enough to create and edit documents. A large number of templates are available in Pages—reports, letters, résumés, envelopes, business cards, flyers, posters, cards, and newsletters— but you may be better off starting with a blank document.

Numbers (http://bit.ly/1gvCGl8) is the tool you'll use for creating spreadsheets, and the iPad version packs a surprising amount of power into a small app. Whether you are a novice or power spreadsheet user, Numbers has something for you. Again, you won't find every feature here that you would on the Mac version, but you can always transfer your document to your computer to modify and improve it.

It seems that **Keynote** (http://bit.ly/1eMZrAl) is an app for which the iPad was specifically built—you can design and create beautiful presentations with it and then use it to show those presentations. Keynote packs some fantastic graphics effects and customizable transitions, as well as a ton of great templates that you can apply with just a few taps. If you rely on notes during your presentations or prefer to use a remote when presenting, Keynote offers a "Keynote Remote" feature built right into the app, which allows you to use your iPhone or iPad as a remote device to control your presentation on another device.

For some, iWork's most glaring drawback (if you consider it a drawback) is its conversion of Microsoft Office documents. For now, anyway, most lawyers still use Word, Excel, and PowerPoint for their productivity needs. But when, for example, you import a PowerPoint file into Keynote on your iPad, you may see that certain fonts are missing or that animations or charts no longer work or look the same. The same is true for Word and Excel files. That's why some of the apps recommended below are better for those of you who still create documents in the world of Microsoft.

The iWork apps *will* export files in their respective Office format so that you can either open documents in other apps or email them to yourself or others.

Documents To Go Premium (http://bit.ly/urrAGu)

The first and second editions of this book featured a pitched battle between Quickoffice (below) and Documents To Go for top word processing suite. In the last edition, Quickoffice came out on top; however, Documents To Go is the clear favorite in this edition, for one primary reason: unlike Quickoffice, Documents To Go Premium allows you to connect to a multitude of cloud services to store or access your documents.

Docs To Go has been around a long time, syncing documents between PDAs, smartphones, and other devices for years. The iPad version comes in two flavors: a basic edition that offers viewing and editing of Word and Excel documents and a Pro release that adds PowerPoint viewing and editing and cloud services support. You can also download the free desktop sync tool, which allows you to pick a folder on your computer and sync the documents inside it to your iPad, or you can sync with iTunes if you prefer.

As far as editing goes, you just get the basics with Docs To Go. You can change the font (only six styles are available), text, or highlight color; indent and justify text; and create bulleted, numbered, or outline text. The point here is document editing, not formatting—you'll want to use your regular desktop application to "pretty up" things. Like many document applications, Docs To Go features an **Open in** option that allows you to open your document in any application on your iPad that supports that file type.

As with most of these applications, Docs To Go has a few shortcomings. The Search feature will only search for document names—you cannot search within documents, although you can search in a specific document itself. Docs To Go also seems more suited for individual users. If you want this app as part of a networked computer environment at your firm or company, check with the IT department to make sure it will work with your current document management systems.

A must-have feature of all document apps is the ability to access files in the cloud, and Documents To Go does not disappoint. You can connect the app to Google Drive, Box, Dropbox, SugarSync, or iCloud and store all of your documents there. All you do is configure the services you want to use with Docs To Go, and they will automatically appear as folders when you are ready to view or edit files on your iPad. There's a Sync feature you can use to make sure the documents on your tablet are the same as the documents on Dropbox; just press the **Sync** button, and all of your changes on the iPad are synced with the cloud. You can also use iTunes to sync your files, but now that you've seen all the great online services that work with these apps, doesn't that seem a bit old-fashioned?

Quickoffice (http://bit.ly/1b91VHS)

Quickoffice has been my favorite word processing app the past few years. In my opinion, the app gives users the best of both worlds: the capabilities of Documents To Go with the user interface of iWork. There's no denying it's much more pleasant to work in than Docs To Go. However, Google acquired the app in 2012, and while it is no longer charging for Quickoffice, you can only sync your documents with Google Drive, which in my opinion is just too limited for this type of app. Further, Quickoffice had not been updated to the new iOS 7 format at the time of this book's publication, so it looks out of date when compared with Documents To

Go. For these reasons, Quickoffice loses to Documents To Go as "Favorite Word Processing App" in this third edition.

Like Docs To Go, the Quickoffice feature set is pretty basic. Aside from the expected bold, italic, and underline functions, you can choose from a number of font styles and sizes, and there are options for paragraph indentation and alignment. But Quickoffice is designed to give you a great iPad experience, easily allowing you to drag and drop files directly from the iPad into your Google Drive account and vice versa. And in that respect, it's a great success.

CloudOn (http://bit.ly/ADL52Z)

Many iPad users complain that tools like Quickoffice and Documents To Go lack the full functionality of the applications found in Microsoft Office: Word, Excel, and PowerPoint. Although Documents To Go will display documents with Track Changes enabled, you cannot actually redline a document. Quickoffice offers a Track Changes feature, but it looks nothing like the Track Changes you might be used to with Microsoft Word. Fortunately, a number of apps offer the opportunity to work directly within Word or Excel, using fully licensed versions of these products. **CloudOn** is my favorite.

CloudOn provides direct access to Office 2010 versions of Word, Excel, and PowerPoint, although in a slightly different way. When you open these applications, you are connecting with them on another computer; therefore, you will need a constant Internet connection if you want to work on files. When you first log in, the applications may look different, too; but don't worry, you are still using MS Word, Excel, and PowerPoint. CloudOn just modified the toolbars to make them easier to use on a tablet.

If you are familiar with Office programs, these will be easy apps to use. They connect to Dropbox, Google Drive, Box, Windows SkyDrive, and Hightail, so you can access your documents from any of these services. Best of all, CloudOn provides access to the full Track Changes features of Microsoft Office. Unfortunately, in late 2013, CloudOn rolled out a Premium service that requires you to pay a monthly or yearly subscription ($7.99 per month, $79.99 per year) if you want to take advantage of features like Track Changes—or basically any feature in MS Office worth using. The free version is essentially no better than Docs To Go or Quickoffice in terms of features, which is a little disappointing.

Additional Options

Other office suite apps.   There are many choices in the App Store for document-creation office suites; the ones mentioned above tend to get the best reviews among lawyers. Good apps also include **Office² HD** (http://bit.ly/1bHoiRw), **Smart Office 2** (http://bit.ly/18Opy8G), and **hopTo** (http://bit.ly/18OpF43).

Google Drive.   Both Documents To Go and Quickoffice can import your Google Docs so you can edit them as you would any other word processing, spreadsheet, or presentation file. But if you don't want to go to the expense of buying these apps, can you just use Google Docs itself on the iPad? The answer is yes—the free Google Drive (http://bit.ly/193KnQ5) app provides access to all your Google Docs and has features similar to the apps mentioned above. So if you are a heavy Google Docs user, the Google Drive app may be all you need.

Microsoft Office web apps.   The giant in the market is obviously Microsoft Office, and for years we have been waiting for dedicated Word, Excel, and PowerPoint apps for the iPad. Unfortunately, we'll probably be waiting a while longer, if not forever. Microsoft just doesn't seem to want to roll out an iPad version of its applications, choosing instead to compete by providing the complete Office suite on Windows Surface tablets. For now, to access Office on your iPad you'll have to use Office Web Apps (http://office.microsoft.com/en-us/web-apps/). The apps are free to use and provide a slimmed-down but still very useful version of the MS Office tools.

There *is* a way to run a full version of Office on your iPad, much like CloudOn. It requires you to learn about something called *application virtualization*, which will take you much longer than the hour you're spending reading this book. But if you're interested in trying it, you'll need three things: (1) a thin-client app such as **Citrix Receiver** (http://bit.ly/rHd52g) running on the iPad, (2) a server-hosted version of Office running in your enterprise data center, and (3) someone from IT to help you connect it, assuming it is compatible with your firm's or company's network. It is neither cheap nor easy for most IT shops to set this up, which is why apps like CloudOn are better options for a pure Office experience on the iPad.

Creating PDFs on your iPad. Not everyone needs to create Word documents on the iPad. Maybe all you need to create is a PDF file so you can annotate or add comments to it. (**Note**: You cannot annotate a Word document on your iPad. To annotate, the document must be a PDF file.) PDF conversion apps are plentiful in the App Store; some of my favorites include **PDF PROvider** (http://bit.ly/1hSMjuR), **PDF Converter** (http://bit.ly/1eoD2bp), and **Snap2PDF** (http://bit.ly/19zFdvp).

A Note on PowerPoint

Most iPad owners use Keynote for creating and delivering presentations. Keynote is a great program, and the iPad version does a good job helping you make interesting and dynamic presentations. I live in the Microsoft Office world, however, so I prefer PowerPoint. Unfortunately, Keynote's conversion of PowerPoint files is less than satisfactory, at least for me; some fonts are replaced with others, and charts and images are moved around. You may find yourself spending a lot of time rebuilding a file once it's converted to Keynote. For a better experience using PowerPoint on the iPad, try **SlideShark** (www.slideshark.com; app at http://bit.ly/LiHrxo). It will render the PowerPoint file exactly as you originally designed it, and you have a number of great options for giving your presentation, including slide annotation, timers, and a place to see your notes, if you keep them. SlideShark is a terrific tool for using PowerPoint on the iPad, and you can't beat the price: free.

Reading on the iPad

After drafting documents, the activity lawyers probably engage in most is reading and annotating documents. Whether you are reading pleadings or discovery from another party, a deposition of an important witness, legal articles from the Internet, important information for an upcoming transaction, or marking up legal research or memos prepared by an associate, reading is likely a fundamental part of your workday.

And because the iPad was primarily designed as a content consumption device, it's extraordinarily well suited for both reading and annotation. In this section we'll cover a few of my favorite apps for reading or marking up any type of document.

Let's start with documents lawyers read every day: pleadings, discovery, correspondence, reports, contracts, case law, and the like. More often than not, you'll be viewing PDF files, but you also want an app that lets you view other document types as well. My two favorite apps for reading documents are GoodReader and PDF Expert.

GoodReader (http://bit.ly/urxFKM) is on everyone's list of must-have iPad apps, and it's easy to see why it should be one of the first you download. It can handle just about any type of file: Office and iWork documents, PDFs, text files, HTML pages, photos, music, and videos. It imports documents using a number of different options, including Wi-Fi, a specific web URL, mail or FTP servers, Google Drive, Dropbox, Sky-Drive, SugarSync, Box—and we're just getting started!

Once you have loaded GoodReader with the documents you want to read, you'll be dealing with two main views: My Documents and the viewing/file management window (see Figure 5.4).

Figure 5.4 GoodReader

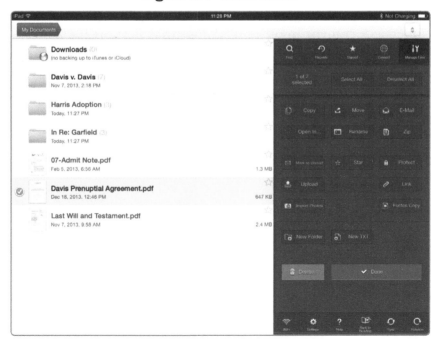

As the name implies, GoodReader does a great job with reading files. But the real value of the app is in its file-management capabilities. As we've discussed, the iPad lacks a coherent filing structure like regular computers. GoodReader helps to alleviate this shortcoming by providing the ability to organize and store files within user-created folders. Even better, you can manage these files in a couple of different ways under the appropriately named Manage Files pane on the right side of the screen. GoodReader also lets you do the following:

- copy or move documents to other folders
- password-protect sensitive files
- attach documents to an email (Apple's Mail app does not permit attachments, so this feature alone justifies GoodReader's cost)
- extract individual files from a PDF portfolio
- rename documents
- create a zip file of multiple files or folders
- open a document in other iPad apps that support it
- create a "to-do" task (requires Appigo's **Todo** app (http://bit.ly/1hr2Ghu) to be installed on the iPad)

And that's not all—the right side of the My Documents screen allows you to preview documents, find files in GoodReader by entering a few keywords, and connect to the online services or web pages you use to download documents.

In the actual document viewing window, you have different options depending on the type of document you're viewing. For example, if you're reading a PDF file, you can change its orientation, crop it, add bookmarks, or even convert it to a text file (if the PDF supports text extraction). GoodReader also allows some annotations: you can highlight, underline, cross out, insert, and replace text, or leave notes.

In all views, you have the ability to send your document to an email address, an AirPrint-compatible printer, or another iPad app that supports it.

GoodReader is fast, solid, and dependable, and it definitely should be a part of your app collection.

If you need to edit a document, you might choose one of the word processing tools above—but if that document is a PDF file, those apps won't work. Instead, you'll want an app that lets you comment on or otherwise annotate the document.

PDF Expert 5 (http://bit.ly/1gCZ9iW) is my app of choice for working on PDF files. If you like to review case law in PDF, then you'll love this product. The functionality is simple but very powerful. There are a dozen ways to get PDF files into the app: through file-sharing services like Dropbox, Box, SugarSync, or Google Drive; an FTP/SFTP server; or other WebDAV server. You can also open files in PDF Expert through other apps that support PDF files, such as GoodReader, Dropbox, and the like.

When you open a PDF file in PDF Expert, there's an annotation toolbar at the top. From the toolbar you can add bookmarks, view outlines and annotations, navigate from page to page, adjust the brightness, send by email, search the file, and open the file in different apps, among other things.

Figure 5.5
Annotation Toolbar

The annotation tools float in a toolbar to the left, and they allow you to do the following (see Figure 5.5):

- add a box, circle, line, or arrow
- highlight text
- underline text
- cross out text
- add a comment
- insert a stamp (select from standard stamps or create your own)
- add text
- write on the document
- insert a signature: you can insert your own saved signature or have a client or someone else sign the document (see Figure 5.6)

Figure 5.6 Inserting a Signature

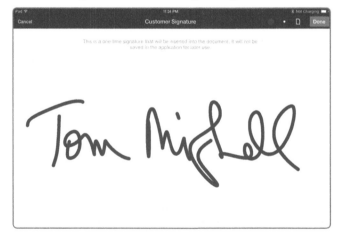

PDF Expert also permits form filling, so you can easily type into forms that are formatted to accept text.

In no time, you'll be marking up case law, pleadings, or other documents that you need to review. When you've finished working on a file, you can move it out of PDF Expert in a couple of ways. If you downloaded the file from your Dropbox account, you can set it up so that the changes are synced automatically back to Dropbox. You can also email, print (using an AirPrint-enabled printer), or open the document in another app that supports PDF files.

With GoodReader and PDF Expert, you've got reading, filing, managing, and marking up documents covered. But what about reading articles and pages you find on the Internet? You can certainly save a web page (in HTML) to GoodReader, but there are better options. My two favorite reading apps are **Instapaper** (http://bit.ly/sQap5s) and **Pocket** (http://bit. ly/1keccXY).

The Pocket app is dead-simple to use, making it easy to save long articles or web pages for later reading, without all the annoying ads and extra junk so often found on the average web page (see Figure 5.7).

Figure 5.7 Pocket

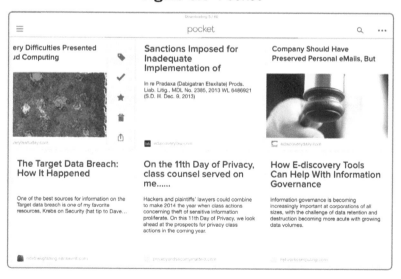

To get started with Pocket, head to www.getpocket.com and sign up for an account. Install the Pocket app on your iPad. You'll be prompted to enter your login credentials once the app launches. If that doesn't happen, tap **Settings** and enter the appropriate information under **Account** to connect to the online version of Pocket.

Next comes a decision: How do you want to save articles to Pocket for reading later? You can save them from your web browser on your computer or iPad. The major browsers all offer extensions to put an **Add to Pocket** button on your toolbar. It's also relatively simple to put Add to Pocket in your Safari bookmarks on your iPad.

You're not limited to using a browser, however, if you want to save articles to Pocket. There are many apps that offer a Send to Pocket feature. To determine if your favorite news app supports Pocket, press the **Share** button in that app or check under **Settings**. All news apps worth having feature the ability to share stories with other apps, and Pocket is typically one of the choices.

Once you've added a few articles to your Pocket queue, head over to the app. You'll see all the articles you've saved, formatted in an easy-to-read layout. After you're done reading an article, you can tag or archive it for later reference, share it by email or a number of social networking sites, save it as a bookmark, open it in your iPad's browser, or even create a blog post with it.

Holding Online Meetings by iPad

If lawyers aren't creating and reading documents, they are meeting with people. These people might be down the hall, across the street, or halfway around the world. In the past few years, online meetings have become more and more popular as the cost of travel has made meeting in person less practical. Fortunately, several companies are making it easy to attend meetings on the iPad; unfortunately, it's still not quite as easy to host your own meeting from the iPad. These apps are my current favorites for online meetings:

- **Fuze** (http://bit.ly/1ccHugd) is currently one of the only meeting apps that allows you to host *and* present a meeting from the iPad. You can use the iPad to listen to audio and add content into the meeting space from your Dropbox account. Premium subscribers have access to multiparty video conferences, recording of meetings, and the ability to host up to 100 attendees.

- **Join.me** (http://bit.ly/1begkPX) is not as full featured as Fuze, but it provides a simple way to share your iPad screen with other meeting attendees. Even better, the service is free and can host up to 250 attendees. The Premium version enables users to host meetings from an iPad and present documents the other attendees can view.

- **GoToMeeting** (http://bit.ly/trm3c7) and Cisco's **WebEx Meetings** (http://bit.ly/1epGJSK) both have great apps for attending meetings, but you cannot host a meeting from either one.

Online meeting tools have come a long way, but apps that lack the ability to host a meeting and show documents just aren't as useful to lawyers.

Brainstorming, Tablet-Style

The last productivity theme we'll cover in this lesson is brainstorming. Lawyers do a lot of that—strategizing on trial tactics, laying out an action plan for an upcoming transaction, or just developing a business plan for a law practice. In recent years mind-mapping software has become a popular way of facilitating the brainstorming process. Wikipedia defines *mind map* as a "diagram used to visually outline information...[,]often created around a single word…to which associated ideas, words, and concepts are added." The iPad has a few good mind-mapping apps available, and in this section we'll discuss two of them.

MindMeister (http://bit.ly/1kWTim2) is a tool I have used on my computer in the past, and I like it quite a bit. It's an offshoot of the mind-mapping website (www.mindmeister.com), but you don't have to have an account there to use the app.

To start a new map, just click the plus sign on the lower left of the screen. Next, click the plus sign in the upper left corner to create a new node, or box that forms part of the map. The keyboard pops up automatically so you can enter text into the node. In the upper right corner, you can access a number of great formatting options by tapping on the paintbrush or paper clip icons; you can format the text size and color, change the box shape and color, insert icons, or change the theme of your map.

Once you're done with your map, you can share it in one of several ways. By choosing **Share Map**, you can provide others with a link to the map on the MindMeister site. When you choose **Export Map**, you can email the mind map in a number of formats: PDF, PNG, RTF, MindMeister, Freemind, MindManager, XMind, Word, or PowerPoint.

A more powerful mind-mapping app is **iThoughtsHD** (http://bit.ly/J6LamH), which has some really great tools. You can use iThoughts to create a map like the one below (see Figure 5.8). Navigation buttons at the top of the screen help you add new nodes to the map. The formatting features are similar to MindMeister, but it's in the saving and exporting of maps where iThoughts really excels. You can send the map by email or Wi-Fi transfer to the camera roll on your iPad, to a cloud-based service like Dropbox or Box, or to a WebDAV server. And there are currently twenty-one file formats to which you can export a map, although many of them are handled by different types of proprietary mind-mapping software.

Figure 5.8 Mind Map Created Using iThoughtsHD

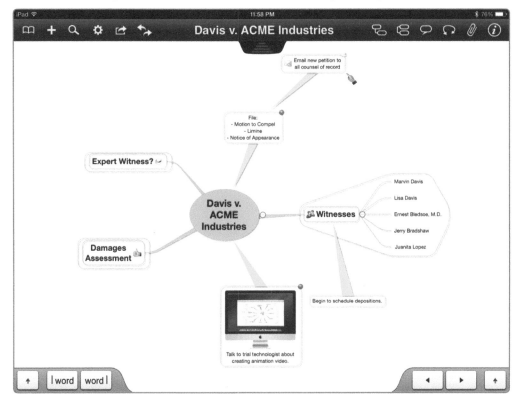

If you like to brainstorm and have never had luck in writing down your ideas, give mind mapping a try. The apps mentioned here, as well as others in the App Store, will make your next brainstorming activity a more pleasurable, or at least a more interesting, experience.

Now that you are on your way to using the iPad in a more productive way, let's take a look at some of the specific legal apps available for your tablet.

Doing Lawyer Things on Your iPad: Legal Apps

So far, we've discussed some of the ways lawyers can use the iPad to be more productive in their practices. In this lesson, we'll look at some legal-specific apps, which help lawyers at trial or doing research. We'll only talk about a few; there are just too many to mention them all. For more legal apps, check out *iPad Apps in One Hour for Lawyers* (ABA, 2012) or *iPad in One Hour for Litigators* (ABA, 2013).

The iPad for Litigators

Of the apps currently available for lawyers, the best ones are designed to help with lawsuits and litigation. When it comes to pretrial apps, my favorite by far is **TranscriptPad** (http://bit.ly/18AOO4d), which is for reviewing and annotating depositions (see Figure 6.1).

Figure 6.1 TranscriptPad

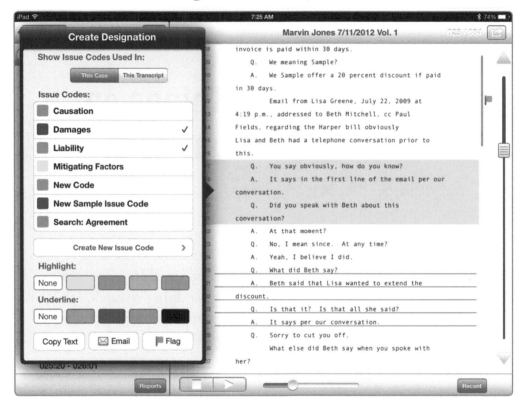

TranscriptPad allows you to create designations for selected testimony; you can annotate the transcript for any issue code you want to create. You can then send those designations in PDF, text, or Excel to your client, co-counsel, or others.

Once you're in the courtroom for trial, the iPad has you covered there as well. When many lawyers pick a jury, they often do so with a legal pad, diagramming the panel to keep track of who is who and who said what. This is where an app like **iJuror** (http://bit.ly/1kXUIgc) comes in handy. Although the design is a little plain, it can hold a lot of information about your jury pool (see Figure 6.2).

Figure 6.2 iJuror

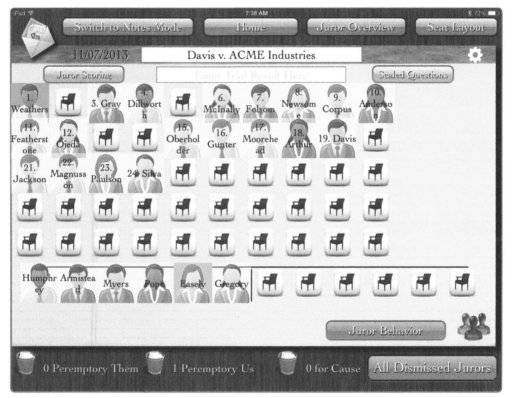

The graphical layout allows you to enter information for each juror, including name, employer, hometown, and other demographic data, such as age, sex, race, marital status, children, education, police in the family, prior arrests, crime victim (or prior plaintiff), and any prior jury experience. You can even perform searches on the panelists on Google and major social network sites with just the push of a button.

While you are questioning jurors, you can rank them based on whether or not you like them or based on a scoring total for each question. Once you've entered all the information, you can just drag and drop the panelists to choose jurors or alternates or dismiss them, indicating the reason for their dismissal.

The Juror Overview page provides a nice all-in-one look at your entire panel, which you can then email to yourself or others for further review or filing.

Although iJuror looks a bit basic, it has most of the features you might want in a juror selection app. Another jury app worth looking at is **JuryPad** (http://bit.ly/JSSyDu) Although these and other jury selection apps are interesting and potentially very useful, they all require a great deal of data input. In my trial experience, I often received jury information just a few minutes before the panel entered the courtroom; there certainly wasn't enough time to enter the information into any of these apps. They might be useful for trials where you receive the jury information well ahead of time or when an assistant is available to perform data entry. Otherwise, they may be more work than they're worth.

Once the trial starts, you'll need technology to present your evidence to the jury. There are half a dozen or so apps that currently handle evidence presentation, and they do so with varying degrees of success. If you are familiar with advanced trial presentation tools like Trial Director or Sanction, you will notice that none of the comparable iPad apps come close in terms of features or functionality. However, the apps do have a place in the courtroom under the right circumstances, depending on the trial, hearing, mediation, or deposition.

My favorite trial presentation app is **TrialPad** (http://bit.ly/1e0HHjN). Setting up a case in TrialPad is easy—simply select the plus sign in the bottom menu of the home screen, and a new folder will pop up for you to name and enter a description. Then it's time to add your documents. TrialPad supports a number of document formats—PDF, MS Office, Apple iWork, and most common image formats, text files, and video files—and unlike other trial presentation apps, it allows you to create video clips. However, I recommend you consider converting all of your document exhibits to PDF, because that format works best with TrialPad (and other trial presentation apps, for that matter). You can add files through a Dropbox or WebDAV account, by using File Sharing in iTunes (see Lesson 4), from your iPad's camera roll, or by opening an email attachment in TrialPad.

You can organize documents by file or by folder on the left side of the screen; just press the plus sign at the bottom of the file area to add a folder. Once you have your documents loaded into TrialPad, you can start organizing them—moving them into different folders by issue, witness, or other criteria. You can also customize your folders with different colors or images. There's a location for multimedia; you can add any video type supported by the iPad, so it's easy to present videos of depositions, accident scenes or reconstructions, or other kinds of video evidence. Finally, the Key Docs area gives you a handy place to access documents particularly important to your case. To add a document here, just press the **Key** button in the upper right corner while viewing that document. Anything you mark as key will appear under Key Docs, which is useful when organizing exhibits for a particular witness or to display to the jury during closing argument.

TrialPad's annotation capabilities are impressive. You can highlight text, draw or write on an exhibit, or use a faux laser pointer to indicate specific parts of a document. If the judge rules a part of your exhibit inadmissible, you can use the redacting tool to blank out that portion. My favorite feature, however, is the callout—this allows you to zoom in on a particular area of an exhibit to show the judge or jury something that needs closer attention. You can use any of the annotation options to mark up your exhibits ahead of time or during presentation at trial or hearing.

When you are ready to present the document, make sure the iPad is properly attached to a projector or high-definition television (via a VGA adapter or Apple TV—both available from the Apple Store). Then move the **Output** button from **OFF** to **ON**. You'll see three different presentation buttons: **Blank**, when you want to show a blank screen; **Freeze**, to show a frozen image of the last exhibit while you work behind the scenes with the next exhibit; and **Present**, to display the current exhibit on-screen. There's also a button at the bottom that allows you to display two documents side by side.

TrialPad is an extremely powerful trial presentation app. It's also the most expensive: $89.99 at the time of this book's publication. However, compared with $500 to $600 per license for products like Sanction or Trial Director, TrialPad is very reasonable considering the power it brings to evidence presentation.

If price *is* an issue, then try the free **TrialDirector for iPad** (http://bit.ly/1jucPPo), a companion to the PC-based trial presentation tool of the same name. It really works best if you are also using the full version of TrialDirector, but for a free app, the presentation tools are decent.

Neither of these apps comes remotely close to the power of the PC-based Sanction or TrialDirector, so they may not be the best tools in cases where you might have huge numbers of documents and lots of synchronized video depositions. But they will do quite well in cases with fewer documents, and they definitely work for hearings, mediations, or other types of presentations.

Legal Research Anywhere

Imagine being able to access your entire law library, wherever you happen to be. At any moment, you have instant access to case law, rules, statutes, and other legal research materials. With the iPad, you can come pretty close to doing that. I have spoken to many lawyers who find it extremely convenient (and in many cases, lifesaving) to be able to immediately look up a case cited in court by opposing counsel, quickly research that case and others, and then respond to the argument without going back to the office. The iPad makes this possible.

If you're a Westlaw or Lexis subscriber, I definitely recommend looking into the **WestlawNext** (http://bit.ly/1gNWfb9) or **Lexis Advance HD** (http://bit.ly/19jwFbY) apps—they both provide excellent research interfaces. Although the apps are free, you must have a Westlaw or Lexis subscription to use them.

Even if you have one of the above apps, I also recommend you download and use **Fastcase** (http://bit.ly/1cJkKPS), the iPad companion to the online service. The app is free, meaning you won't be getting as many features as you might if you signed up for a paid subscription. However, the free case law search may be all you need at a specific moment. Further, many of you may live in states where Fastcase is provided as a bar association member benefit; check to see whether use of the Fastcase app is included free as part of that membership.

To search with Fastcase, select **New Search** and then choose whether you want to search case law or statutes. For case law searches, enter your search terms or citation. Federal cases from all courts (Supreme, circuit, district, and bankruptcy) are available, as well as case law from all fifty states. You can filter your search by jurisdiction and date range, and you can opt to have your results check authorities for cases citing and cited by a specific case. You can go through your results and save them. That's about all you can do with the free version.

If you upgrade to the premium edition of Fastcase, you get a number of additional useful features, including:

- unlimited customer support
- dual-column printing of documents
- more powerful sorting tools
- ability to email a case or search results

- visual maps of search results
- access to more libraries, such as court rules, administrative regulations, and constitutions
- newspaper search, people finder, business intelligence, and forms
- unified search within PACER (one search for all courts)

To get all of this, you'll have to subscribe to one of the Fastcase services, which at the time of this book's publication were between $65 and $95 per month, depending on the plan. But for fast, mobile legal research, the free version is a great app, as long as you understand the limitations.

One other legal research app that I consider a must-have provides you with access to the statutes and rules of your particular state or jurisdiction. The problem is, there are a lot of apps offering statutes and rules for different states, at differing levels of quality. One app that claims to provide à la carte access to the rules and statutes of *almost* all fifty states is **AllLaw** (http://bit.ly/1juluBb). My personal favorite is **LawBox** (http://bit.ly/1a0tIr1), which bills itself as your "mobile law library." It's a great app, but only provides statutes and rules for seven states, plus federal codes and rules. As with AllLaw, you'll have to purchase each title, typically for $4.99 each. (If you are a member of the State Bar of Texas, you can subscribe to the Computer and Technology Law Section and get a specially customized version of the app with all Texas law for free.) Let's hope that LawBox adds more states in the future.

Another great feature of LawBox is its Annotations page. When you are viewing a rule or statute, just press the **Annotations** button, and Google Scholar will search all case law that mentions it. You'll then have access to the full case through the excellent Google Scholar service.

If you want to see if there is something better for your particular state, just go to the App Store and type in *Law [Name of State]*, and you'll see a list of every app that might have statutes or rules for your jurisdiction.

As I mention elsewhere in this book, it's hard to keep up with new apps because they're coming out all the time. If the legal-specific software you currently use on your computer isn't yet available in an iPad app, keep checking—legal technology vendors are all scrambling to roll out mobile versions of their software offerings.

The Ever-Changing Nature of Technology

Why Parts of This Book May Seem Out of Date

The challenge of writing a book about technology is that it's always changing—the technology, that is. Between editions of this book, developers add new features to apps that are mentioned, and some apps are no longer being updated. Even more important, Apple continues to release new versions of the iPad, introducing additional bells and whistles and improving existing functionality.

By the time you read this book, many things may have changed with the iPad or the apps you install on it. New features may have been added or existing ones removed; a button that was on the left might now be on the right. Apps are constantly being updated—features can come and go with dizzying frequency. The descriptions for certain apps that I've included may be different by the time you read this book, and new app releases might correct particular issues I mention. In other words, your mileage may vary. I'm blogging at *iPad 4 Lawyers* (http://ipad4lawyers. squarespace.com), where I review new apps and provide tips on how to get the most out of your tablet—be sure to check there regularly for the latest iPad information.

Security on Your iPad

When you first set up your iPad (see Introduction), one of the first things to do is make sure your security settings are properly configured. Given the portability of the device, it's very easy to leave an iPad on a plane, in a taxi, or in your hotel room, and computing devices are always in danger of theft. To configure the security options, press **Settings** and then **General**. Press **Passcode Lock** first.

- By default, the **Simple Passcode** option is switched **ON** to allow you to configure a four-digit passcode. If you want a longer, more secure passcode (and I *strongly* suggest this), move the setting to **OFF** and follow the instructions below. The current recommended minimum length for a password is *twelve characters*, with a combination of uppercase and lowercase letters, numbers, and symbols.

- Press the **Turn Passcode On** button, and you'll be prompted to enter a passcode—either four digits or longer, depending upon whether **Simple Passcode** is set to **ON**. Enter your passcode once, then enter it again for confirmation. Now your passcode is set.

- The **Require Passcode** option forces you to enter your passcode after the iPad has been idle for a certain period of time. You can set this option for immediately or for one, five, or fifteen minutes. I recommend the five-minute setting, which gives you reasonable protection without the constant need to enter your passcode.

- Consider whether you want to allow access to Siri when the iPad is locked. Moving this option to **ON** will allow others to control apps on your iPad simply by using Siri, even if they do not know your passcode. Choose carefully.

- When you move the **Erase Data** option to the **ON** position, all data on your iPad is erased after ten failed attempts at entering the passcode. I recommend you enable this setting.

If your iPad is lost or stolen, you can still protect it from afar. If you've just bought a new iPad, one of the setup questions should be "Do you want to enable Find My iPhone?" If not, go to the App Store and download the free **Find My iPhone** (http://bit.ly/1g4y4SR) app (don't worry, it works for the iPad, too). Once it's installed, log in to your Apple account, and the app will display a map showing where your iPad is at that very moment—as long as it's turned on and connected to the Internet. So you may need to try several times before you can locate the device. Once you do, you have a few options: you can make it play a sound (useful if the iPad is nearby); you can enable Lost Mode, which will lock the iPad and provide contact information in case someone finds it; or you can erase all the data on it. You can access Find My iPhone from any Apple device or at www.icloud.com; just enter your Apple ID.

Consider these additional security options:

- **Encrypt your data.** When you back up your data in iTunes, you have the option of encryption. Connect your iPad to iTunes, click on the **Summary** tab, and scroll to **Options** at the bottom. Select **Encrypt iPad** and then set (or change) your password.
- **Use a VPN.** Although it may not be for everyone, a Virtual Private Network (VPN) provides a secure connection when you are using the device. First, you need to find a VPN connection; one great option is **proXPN** (www.proxpn.com). There's a free version, but the paid service provides strong security at a reasonable price. You can also use an app like **Cisco AnyConnect** (http://bit.ly/1crCgLU), which can set up a VPN for you; go to the App Store and search for VPN. Once you have a VPN tool, then go to **Settings > Network > VPN**,

and enter the settings given by your VPN provider.

- **Disable Bluetooth.** If you're not using your Bluetooth connection, make sure it's turned off. Press **Settings** > **General** > **Bluetooth**.

- **Enable Safari's security settings.** Consider whether you need to do this. If you do, press **Settings** > **Safari** and check the following settings:

  - Block Pop-Ups: **ON**

  - Do Not Track: Move to **ON** if you do not want Safari to keep track of your browsing history.

  - Block Cookies: Specify if or when you want to save cookies in the browser.

  - Fraudulent Website Warning: **ON**

  - Clear History, Cookies, Data: It's a good idea to periodically clear your browser of these items.

Finger Moves and Shortcuts

Finger Moves

You can use several different finger moves on the iPad to accomplish certain tasks. Here are the main finger moves and what each does:

- **Tap.** With the tip of your finger, directly touch what you see on screen; it can be an icon, song title, or app control. You don't need to push hard—a gentle press is all it takes. You tap when you want to select something.

   - **Double-tap.** In some apps it's an easy way to zoom in quickly. In videos it can be used to toggle between full-screen and wide-screen view.

   - Although it's not a tap, if you double-*click* the **Home** button, it brings up the **App Switcher**, which lets you easily move between open apps.

- **Drag.** Keep your finger pressed on the screen and slide it around to scroll to different parts of the screen. This move helps you set volume sliders or pan around objects larger than the screen. You can also try out the two-finger drag to scroll in a window that's within another window.

- **Slide.** It's almost like a drag, but you only use the slide in one case: to interact with the iPad's **Slide to Unlock/Slide to Power Off** buttons, which is where you wake your iPad or confirm a shutdown of the device.

- **Swipe.** By lightly whipping your finger up or down the screen, you can make a web page, song list, or other long page zip by in the direction of your flick. Here are some other swipe moves you can make with one or more fingers:
  - One finger:
    - Swipe down from anywhere on your home screen to reveal the Spotlight Search box, which allows you to search everything stored on your iPad.
    - Swipe down from the top of the screen to reveal the Notification Center.
    - Swipe up from the bottom of the screen to reveal the Control Center (see Lesson 1).
  - Two fingers:
    - To zoom in on part of a page or picture, take your thumb and index finger, put them on the screen where you want to zoom, and spread them out across the glass. To zoom out, do the same thing, but this time pinch your thumb and index finger together.
  - Four fingers:
    - Swipe up to show the App Switcher, thumbnails of all open apps, so you can easily switch from one app to another.
    - Swipe to the left or right to quickly move between apps that are currently open.

Shortcuts: Cut, Copy, Paste

All of these commands are in the same menu.

- First, double-tap the word or sentence you want to cut or copy; in some apps you may need to use a long press instead of a double-tap. A box will pop up, and depending on the app, it will give some combination of options. For example, in email you've received it's **Copy | Select All | Define**, but in an email you're composing, you'll see **Cut | Copy | Paste | Replace | B/U | Define | Quote Level | Insert Photo or Video** (whew!).

- A blue highlight will appear around the word or sentence with dots on each end; to select more words, sentences, or a whole paragraph, drag the dots to expand the highlighting.

- Tap the command you want to use (depending on the box you see).

- If you want to paste, double-tap the spot where you want to paste. A **Paste** button will pop up. Tap the button to insert the text or photo into its new location.

Keyboard Shortcuts

- Need an accent on that *e* or other letter? Press and hold the letter you are typing (*a, c, e, i, l, n, o, s, u, y,* or *z*), and you'll see a number of different choices for that letter.

- Tap the space bar twice to add a period to the end of a sentence.

- You can also force keys to appear on the main keyboard that aren't originally there. For example, to get to an apostrophe or quotation marks, you typically have to press the **.?123** key. But if you just press down the comma (,) button and slide, you'll see the apostrophe appear above. Try the same thing with the period (.) button, and quotation marks will appear. (In a web browser, pressing on the period button will bring up a list of domains when you are trying to type a website URL: .org, .net, etc.)

- The iPad's AutoCorrect feature is both a blessing and a curse. It will automatically correct your bad typing, which can be great. But if you're not paying attention, it can also substitute a completely different word for what you originally intended. Here are two tips for dealing with AutoCorrect:

- As you are typing a word, AutoCorrect may pop up an alternate suggestion. If that's the word you want, simply touch the space bar and keep going—the word will be accepted and inserted where you are typing. If you don't like the suggested correction, just tap it to make it go away.

- If you don't look at the text when you type, you might miss words that are inserted by AutoCorrect. To prevent this, go to **Settings** > **General** > **Accessibility** > **Speak Auto-Text**. From now on, your iPad will speak when it makes an Auto-Correct suggestion.

- Go to **Settings** > **General** > **Keyboard** to turn other shortcuts on or off:

  - **Auto-Capitalization.** This feature will automatically capitalize the first letter after a period.

  - **Enable Caps Lock.** When you double-tap the **Shift** key, it turns blue, and you can type in ALL CAPS until you tap **Shift** again to turn it off.

  - **"." Shortcut.** If you turn this on, every time you double-tap the space bar, the iPad will insert a period followed by a space.

  - From the Keyboard menu you can also add non-English keyboards, create shortcuts that can help save time when typing, or enable the **Split Keyboard** (see below), which is a great alternative to working with the full keyboard.

Tip: You can create your own text shortcuts on the iPad, too. Go to **Settings** > **General** > **Keyboard** > **Shortcuts** > **Add New Shortcut**. Enter a text cue for a phrase you use often (for example, OMW for "on my way"), and then press **Save**. Now when you type the shortcut, the iPad will automatically insert the phrase for you.

If the iPad's full-screen keyboard is too big, you can reduce its size by splitting it apart. Go to **Settings** > **General** > **Keyboard** and make sure **Split Keyboard** is set to **On**. Next, open an app where you want to type, and when the keyboard pops up, place your thumbs in the center of it and then move them apart, literally "splitting" the keyboard. You'll now see half of your keyboard on each side of the screen, which is pretty easy to navigate using just your thumbs.

Using Siri

When you press and hold on the **Home** button, you activate **Siri**, Apple's intelligent digital assistant. There are plenty of fun things you can do with Siri (just ask Siri to tell you a joke or "How much wood could a woodchuck chuck?"), but there are many useful things this feature can do. Here's a short list of the some of the great ways Siri can serve as your iPad personal assistant (examples of voice commands are in parentheses).

- turn features on or off ("Turn off Bluetooth," or "turn on Wi-Fi.")
- listen to email or other messages ("Read me the last email from Tim Cook.")
- get contact information ("What is Bill Gates's phone number?")
- create calendar events ("Set up a meeting with Michael at 9:00 a.m. tomorrow.")
- change calendar events ("Reschedule my appointment with Michael to Thursday at 4:00 p.m.")
- ask about events ("What's on my calendar for Friday?")
- set alarms ("Wake me up tomorrow at 6:00 a.m.")
- set a timer ("Set the timer for 45 minutes.")
- send email or text messages ("Send an email to Debbie [dictate email].")
- check and respond to email messages ("Read my new email messages.")
- ask for maps and directions ("How do I get from here to the courthouse?")

- ask about local businesses ("Show me the closest Starbucks.")
- set reminders ("Remind me to call Connie Client tomorrow.")
- check the weather for your town or others ("What's the forecast for Boston tomorrow?")
- search the web ("Search for news about the latest Supreme Court decision.")
- post to social media accounts ("Post on Facebook [dictate post]," or "post on Twitter [dictate post].")
- ask a question using Wolfram Alpha ("What's a 20 percent tip on $86.74 for four people?")

You can also dictate documents using Siri. Just open the app where you want to dictate (email, document creation, etc.), press the microphone button next to the space bar, and start talking. Press **Done** when you are finished. This function works best for small chunks of text—don't dictate an entire brief at once.

Accessibility Features

With each new version of the iPad, we see more and more features to help people with disabilities use the device. Some of these tools are beneficial to everyone. Here's a rundown of the assistive capabilities available on the iPad, which you can find by going to **Settings** > **General** > **Accessibility**.

Vision

- When **VoiceOver** is turned on, it will say the items on a screen. There are a *lot* of different options here, including adjusting the speaking rate, using sound effects, choosing a "compact voice," selecting a desired dialect, setting a large cursor, and much more. You can also configure your iPad to work with a Braille device.

- **Zoom** magnifies the entire screen when you double-tap three fingers.

- **Invert Colors** changes the screen to dark and text to white, if the brightness of the screen makes items hard to read.

- If you turn **Speak Selection** on, a **Speak** button will appear whenever you select a block of text.

- **Speak Auto-Text** will speak your auto-corrections and auto-capitalizations.

- If an app supports **Dynamic Type**, you can use the **Larger Type** feature to adjust to your preferred reading size.

- **Bold Text** will automatically bold all text.

- **Increase Contrast** improves the contrast on some backgrounds to increase the legibility of text.

- The new iOS 7 has a few special effects that can make some people dizzy. Turning **Reduce Motion** on will lessen the motion of the user interface.

- **On/Off Labels** adds a | (for **ON**) and an ○ (for **OFF**) to the **On/Off** button.

Hearing

- **Hearing Aids** will connect a hearing aid with Bluetooth capability to the iPad.

- **Subtitles & Captioning** allows closed captioning. You can specify a predesigned style or create your own.

- When **Mono Audio** is on, both channels of audio will play in both ears.

- A balance slider allows you to adjust the volume between left and right speakers.

Learning

- **Guided Access** keeps the iPad in a single app and allows you to control which features are available.

Physical and Motor

- **Switch Control** helps you control the iPad using a single switch or multiple switches. There are lots of customization options here.

- **AssistiveTouch** allows you to use your iPad if you have difficulty touching the screen or if you require an adaptive accessory. You can also create your own gestures to automate functions on the iPad with a swipe or touch.

- **Home Click Speed** adjusts the speed required to double- and triple-click the **Home** button.

- **Accessibility Shortcut** configures what happens when you triple-click the **Home** button. Options are VoiceOver, Invert Colors, Zoom, Switch Control, or AssistiveTouch.

Advanced Email Options

In Lesson 2, I covered the basics of setting up your email, calendar, and contacts. But there are many more ways to configure email on your iPad, and they could definitely use a little explanation. Here's a brief description of the other options you have under **Mail, Contacts, Calendars** in **Settings**.

If you use email from a service other than Exchange, Gmail, Yahoo!, AOL, or Outlook.com, you can set it up under the **Other** option when you add an email account. To do that, go to **Settings** > **Mail, Contacts, Calendars** > **Add Account**. Press the **Other** button to get started.

- **Mail: Add Mail Account.** Press this button to add an email account from a service other than the ones listed above. Then enter your name, email address, password, and an optional description.

- **Contacts: Add LDAP Account.** If your firm or office uses an LDAP (Lightweight Directory Access Protocol) server, press this button and add the LDAP server name and your username, password, and an optional description to access your contacts.

- **Contacts: Add CardDAV Account.** CardDAV is an address book client that allows users to access and share contact data on a server. If you want to add your CardDAV contacts, press this button and enter the CardDAV server name and your username, password, and an optional description.

- **Calendar: Add CalDAV Account.** A CalDAV account is similar to the CardDAV account but for calendar items. If you use a CalDAV account, press this button and add the CalDAV server name and your username, password, and an optional description.

• **Calendar: Add Subscribed Calendar.** A subscribed calendar is a calendar with the .ics (Internet Connection Sharing) extension. It lets users connect to calendars across the Internet without using one of the mail services described above. For example, the TripIt travel service allows you to subscribe to an iCalendar feed of all your upcoming travel plans. To add an iCalendar subscription to your iPad, just choose this option and enter the server or subscription address.

You can also set up **Mail, Contacts, Calendars** through iTunes. With your iPad plugged in to your computer, open iTunes, go to the left menu bar, and click on **iPad** to view the specific options (see Figure A.1).

Figure A.1 Setting Up Mail, Contacts, Calendars in iTunes

Click on **Info**. You'll see ways to sync your contacts, calendar, and mail to the iPad. Curiously, you don't get as many choices here as within the iPad's settings itself. You only get the following:

- **Contacts.** Outlook and Windows Contacts
- **Calendar.** Outlook only
- **Mail.** Outlook only
- **Bookmarks.** Internet Explorer only
- **Notes.** Outlook only

One major benefit of using iTunes to configure these is that you can identify specific groups of contacts, individual calendars, or particular email accounts you want to sync. You don't get that kind of customization with the iPad's internal settings.

Once you have set up your email account, go back to the **Mail, Contacts, Calendars** main page to configure additional options (see Figure A.2).

Figure A.2 Main Screen: Mail, Contacts, Calendars

- **Mail: Fetch New Data.** You can choose to either **Push** or **Fetch** new email messages. With Push, a connection is opened whenever a message is available to deliver. Fetch opens a connection at specific predefined intervals—every fifteen, thirty, or sixty minutes, or you can elect a manual fetch. On the **Fetch New Data** page, you can configure Push/Fetch options for each individual account—although some accounts may not have Push options.

- **Mail: Preview.** Specify how many lines of type (from zero to five) appear as a preview of your email.

- **Mail: Show To/Cc Label.** This feature, when turned on, will display a small To or Cc label on each email in the mail list (in Landscape mode) to denote whether you are the primary recipient or are simply being copied on the message.

- **Mail: Flag Style.** If you flag your email to come back to it later, you can designate different shapes and colors for the flag.

- **Mail: Ask Before Deleting.** With this on, you'll see a **Delete** button that you must press to confirm each deletion of a message. Otherwise, the email will be deleted with a simple swipe of the finger. The button is helpful if your finger tends to accidentally delete the wrong message.

- **Mail: Load Remote Images.** If your email messages have images in them, turning on this option will allow the images to be downloaded and viewed in your email.

- **Mail: Organize by Thread.** This allows you to view the entire thread of an email conversation at once. Instead of being spread throughout a long list, the email messages in a threaded conversation stay together. When you press on a message, you'll get a sublist of the other messages in the conversation.

- **Mail: Always Bcc Myself.** Select this if you like to keep extra copies of the emails you send—it will insert your email address into the Bcc field of all messages you compose.

- **Mail: Increase Quote Level.** Leaving this option on will add a level of indentation when you forward or reply to a message.

- **Mail: Signature.** Here you can specify the signature you want to appear at the bottom of every message. The default is "Sent from my iPad," which you may want to change if you are using the iPad for business purposes. You can use the same signature for all email accounts or have a different signature per account.

- **Mail: Default Account.** If you have multiple email accounts configured, the iPad will require that one account be designated the default for all messages created outside of **Mail**. For example, if you try to mail a news article from apps like Feedly or Pocket, the message will be sent from your default account. (Note: You can easily change the **From** email address on a message-by-message basis—just press on the email address in the **From** line and your other email addresses will appear.)

- **Contacts: Sort Order.** Specify how you want your contacts sorted—First Name/Last Name, or Last Name/First Name.

- **Contacts: Display Order.** Use the same sorting options to specify how you want your contacts displayed.

- **Contacts: Short Name.** To fit more names on the screen, the iPad will display a "Short Name" for each contact. You can choose First Name/Last Initial, First Initial/Last Name, First Name Only, or Last Name Only.

- **Contacts: My Info.** Personalize your iPad by inserting your own contact information here.

- **Contacts: Default Account.** As with email, you must select a default email account for newly created contacts.

- **Calendars: New Invitation Alerts.** Do you want to be alerted as new calendar items are delivered to you? If so, leave this option on.

- **Calendars: Time Zone Support.** When turned on, dates and times are shown in the time zone you set (see Lesson 1). When turned off, events will display in the time zone of your current location.

- **Calendars: Sync.** To save space, this feature allows you to set how far back events should be included on your iPad. Your options are 2 Weeks Back, 1 Month Back, 3 Months Back, 6 Months Back, or All Events.

- **Calendars: Default Alert Times.** You can receive an alert before specific types of events (Birthdays, Events, or All-Day Events). The time of the alert differs based on the type of event.

- **Calendars: Start Week On.** Define the day on which your week starts.

- **Calendars: Default Calendar.** Select a default calendar to which new events will always be posted.

- **Calendars: Shared Calendar Alerts.** If you share calendar items with other people, turn this option on to be notified about new, modified, or deleted events.

My Top Ten Apps

One look through Apple's App Store and you can see that there are a *whole lot of apps* available for the iPad. In the book *iPad Apps in One Hour for Lawyers* (ABA, 2012), I tried to list the two hundred or so that lawyers might find most useful, and you'll find reviews and recommendations at my *iPad 4 Lawyers* blog (http://ipad4lawyers.squarespace.com). Here, I'll just list my top ten must-haves: the iPad apps I think every lawyer should own.

But first, a few words about using the App Store. Apps are the lifeblood of your iPad, and the App Store is where you can get a transfusion. You can download apps in two ways: (1) directly from iTunes or (2) through the App Store icon on your iPad. We'll use the iPad App Store for purposes of our discussion (see Figure A.3).

Figure A.3 iPad App Store

Across the bottom of the screen you have five options:

- **Featured.** Special apps highlighted by the App Store
- **Top Charts.** The most popular paid and free apps in the App Store
- **Near Me.** Apps that are popular near your current location
- **Purchased.** A list of apps you've purchased (You can toggle between All Apps or purchased apps that are not on your iPad. You can also search within your purchased apps.)
- **Updates.** A list of all the available updates for your apps

Use one of the above-mentioned options to start looking for apps. You can also use the Search box (in the upper right corner) and enter keywords. When you find an app you like, press the price tag (or the **Free** button), then press the **Buy** or **Install** button. Enter your iTunes password, and the app will automatically be downloaded and installed.

If you get tired of an app and are ready to get rid of it, there are again two ways to do so: within the iPad or within iTunes.

- To delete an app within your iPad, just press and hold the icon until it begins to jiggle. Press the **X** in the left corner, and you'll be prompted to confirm the deletion. (Remember: if you delete an app from the iPad, you also delete any files you may have created within the app.)
- After opening iTunes on your computer, connect your iPad and then navigate to **iPad** in the left-hand menu. Click the **Apps** tab and uncheck the boxes next to the apps you don't want. They will be removed on the next sync. To remove an app permanently, right-click on it and select **Delete**. Then to make sure it is gone forever, confirm with **Remove Files from Computer** in the next dialog box. (To permanently delete the app, you must delete it within iTunes. If you only delete the app within your iPad, the next time you sync it with iTunes, the app will be reinstalled on your device.)

Tom's Top Ten Apps

Here are the ten apps (or types of apps) I think all lawyers should have on their iPads:

1. **GoodReader** (http://bit.ly/urxFKM). This app offers the best way to manage files and documents on your iPad, as well as read them.

2. **A news reader.** Keeping up with the news in your areas of interest is easy on the iPad. My personal favorite news reader is **Mr. Reader** (http://bit.ly/1ggDDOc); I think it is the most powerful and easiest to use. Other good apps include **Feedly Reader** (http://bit.ly/JFmZvI), **Reeder 2** (http://bit.ly/1em6vms), and **Flipboard** (http://bit.ly/1h9iKHS).

3. **Pocket** (http://bit.ly/1keccXY). This app is a great way to read articles and web pages on a tablet.

4. **Evernote** (http://bit.ly/19xc1VR). I use this as my "personal memory" on my iPad as well as all my other devices. It holds articles, notes, and snippets of information I find and want to keep.

5. **TrialPad** (http://bit.ly/1e0HHjN). This is currently the best evidence presentation app for the iPad.

6. **Fastcase** (http://bit.ly/1cJkKPS). Having free access to case law and statutes on your iPad is a no-brainer.

7. **Noteshelf** (http://bit.ly/1b6HPyS). This is my favorite note-taking app because it's easy to use and full of great features.

8. **Documents To Go Premium** (http://bit.ly/urrAGu). If you work on MS Office files on your iPad, this app provides the best functionality.

9. **PDF Expert** (http://bit.ly/1gCZ9iW). Get this app if you want the best feature set for reviewing and annotating PDF files.

10. **Remember The Milk** (http://bit.ly/19WiVlD). This is my favorite to-do list app; I use it on the iPad almost as much as on my desktop and laptop.

Index

SELECTED BOOKS FROM THE LAW PRACTICE DIVISION

LinkedIn in One Hour for Lawyers, Second Edition
By Dennis Kennedy and Allison C. Shields

Product Code: 5110773 • LPM Price: $39.95 • Regular Price: $49.95

Since the first edition of LinkedIn in One Hour for Lawyers was published, LinkedIn has added almost 100 million users, and more and more lawyers are using the platform on a regular basis. Now, this bestselling ABA book has been fully revised and updated to reflect significant changes to LinkedIn's layout and functionality made through 2013. LinkedIn in One Hour for Lawyers, Second Edition, will help lawyers make the most of their online professional networking. In just one hour, you will learn to:

- Set up a LinkedIn® account
- Create a robust, dynamic profile--and take advantage of new multimedia options
- Build your connections
- Get up to speed on new features such as Endorsements, Influencers, Contacts, and Channels
- Enhance your Company Page with new functionality
- Use search tools to enhance your network
- Monitor your network with ease
- Optimize your settings for privacy concerns
- Use LinkedIn® effectively in the hiring process
- Develop a LinkedIn strategy to grow your legal network

Blogging in One Hour for Lawyers
By Ernie Svenson

Product Code: 5110744 • LPM Price: $24.95 • Regular Price: $39.95

Until a few years ago, only the largest firms could afford to engage an audience of millions. Now, lawyers in any size firm can reach a global audience at little to no cost—all because of blogs. An effective blog can help you promote your practice, become more "findable" online, and take charge of how you are perceived by clients, journalists and anyone who uses the Internet. Blogging in One Hour for Lawyers will show you how to create, maintain, and improve a legal blog—and gain new business opportunities along the way. In just one hour, you will learn to:

- Set up a blog quickly and easily
- Write blog posts that will attract clients
- Choose from various hosting options like Blogger, TypePad, and WordPress
- Make your blog friendly to search engines, increasing your ranking
- Tweak the design of your blog by adding customized banners and colors
- Easily send notice of your blog posts to Facebook and Twitter
- Monitor your blog's traffic with Google Analytics and other tools
- Avoid ethics problems that may result from having a legal blog

The Electronic Evidence and Discovery Handbook: Forms, Checklists, and Guidelines
By Sharon D. Nelson, Bruce A. Olson, and John W. Simek

Product Code: 5110569 • LPM Price: $99.95 • Regular Price: $129.95

The use of electronic evidence has increased dramatically over the past few years, but many lawyers still struggle with the complexities of electronic discovery. This substantial book provides lawyers with the templates they need to frame their discovery requests and provides helpful advice on what they can subpoena. In addition to the ready-made forms, the authors also supply explanations to bring you up to speed on the electronic discovery field. The accompanying CD-ROM features over 70 forms, including, Motions for Protective Orders, Preservation and Spoliation Documents, Motions to Compel, Electronic Evidence Protocol Agreements, Requests for Production, Internet Services Agreements, and more. Also included is a full electronic evidence case digest with over 300 cases detailed!

Facebook® in One Hour for Lawyers
By Dennis Kennedy and Allison C. Shields

Product Code: 5110745 • LPM Price: $24.95 • Regular Price: $39.95

With a few simple steps, lawyers can use Facebook® to market their services, grow their practices, and expand their legal network—all by using the same methods they already use to communicate with friends and family. Facebook® in One Hour for Lawyers will show any attorney—from Facebook® novices to advanced users—how to use this powerful tool for both professional and personal purposes.

Android Apps in One Hour for Lawyers
By Daniel J. Siegel

Product Code: 5110754 • LPM Price: $19.95 • Regular Price: $34.95

Lawyers are already using Android devices to make phone calls, check e-mail, and send text messages. After the addition of several key apps, Android smartphones or tablets can also help run a law practice. From the more than 800,000 apps currently available, Android Apps in One Hour for Lawyers highlights the "best of the best" apps that will allow you to practice law from your mobile device. In just one hour, this book will describe how to buy, install, and update Android apps, and help you:

- Store documents and files in the cloud
- Use security apps to safeguard client data on your phone
- Be organized and productive with apps for to-do lists, calendar, and contacts
- Communicate effectively with calling, text, and e-mail apps
- Create, edit, and organize your documents
- Learn on the go with news, reading, and reference apps
- Download utilities to keep your device running smoothly
- Hit the road with apps for travel
- Have fun with games and social media apps

SELECTED BOOKS FROM THE LAW PRACTICE DIVISION

Virtual Law Practice:
How to Deliver Legal Services Online
By Stephanie L. Kimbro

Product Code: 5110707 • **LPM Price:** $47.95 • **Regular Price:** $79.95

The legal market has recently experienced a dramatic shift as lawyers seek out alternative methods of practicing law and providing more affordable legal services. Virtual law practice is revolutionizing the way the public receives legal services and how legal professionals work with clients. If you are interested in this form of practicing law, *Virtual Law Practice* will help you:

- Responsibly deliver legal services online to your clients
- Successfully set up and operate a virtual law office
- Establish a virtual law practice online through a secure, client-specific portal
- Manage and market your virtual law practice
- Understand state ethics and advisory opinions
- Find more flexibility and work/life balance in the legal profession

Social Media for Lawyers: The Next Frontier
By Carolyn Elefant and Nicole Black

Product Code: 5110710 • **LPM Price:** $47.95 • **Regular Price:** $79.95

The world of legal marketing has changed with the rise of social media sites such as Linkedin, Twitter, and Facebook. Law firms are seeking their companies attention with tweets, videos, blog posts, pictures, and online content. Social media is fast and delivers news at record pace. This book provides you with a practical, goal-centric approach to using social media in your law practice that will enable you to identify social media platforms and tools that fit your practice and implement them easily, efficiently, and ethically.

iPad Apps in One Hour for Lawyers
By Tom Mighell

Product Code: 5110739 • **LPM Price:** $19.95 • **Regular Price:** $34.95

At last count, there were more than 80,000 apps available for the iPad. Finding the best apps often can be an overwhelming, confusing, and frustrating process. iPad Apps in One Hour for Lawyers provides the "best of the best" apps that are essential for any law practice. In just one hour, you will learn about the apps most worthy of your time and attention. This book will describe how to buy, install, and update iPad apps, and help you:

- Find apps to get organized and improve your productivity
- Create, manage, and store documents on your iPad
- Choose the best apps for your law office, including litigation and billing apps
- Find the best news, reading, and reference apps
- Take your iPad on the road with apps for travelers
- Maximize your social networking power
- Have some fun with game and entertainment apps during your relaxation time

Twitter in One Hour for Lawyers
By Jared Correia

Product Code: 5110746 • **LPM Price:** $24.95 • **Regular Price:** $39.95

More lawyers than ever before are using Twitter to network with colleagues, attract clients, market their law firms, and even read the news. But to the uninitiated, Twitter's short messages, or tweets, can seem like they are written in a foreign language. Twitter in One Hour for Lawyers will demystify one of the most important social-media platforms of our time and teach you to tweet like an expert. In just one hour, you will learn to:

- Create a Twitter account and set up your profile
- Read tweets and understand Twitter jargon
- Write tweets—and send them at the appropriate time
- Gain an audience—follow and be followed
- Engage with other Twitters users
- Integrate Twitter into your firm's marketing plan
- Cross-post your tweets with other social media platforms like Facebook and LinkedIn
- Understand the relevant ethics, privacy, and security concerns
- Get the greatest possible return on your Twitter investment
- And much more!

The Lawyer's Essential Guide to Writing
By Marie Buckley

Product Code: 5110726 • **LPM Price:** $47.95 • **Regular Price:** $79.95

This is a readable, concrete guide to contemporary legal writing. Based on Marie Buckley's years of experience coaching lawyers, this book provides a systematic approach to all forms of written communication, from memoranda and briefs to e-mail and blogs. The book sets forth three principles for powerful writing and shows how to apply those principles to develop a clean and confident style.

iPad in One Hour for Lawyers, Second Edition
By Tom Mighell

Product Code: 5110747 • **LPM Price:** $24.95 • **Regular Price:** $39.95

Whether you are a new or a more advanced iPad user, *iPad in One Hour for Lawyers* takes a great deal of the mystery and confusion out of using your iPad. Ideal for lawyers who want to get up to speed swiftly, this book presents the essentials so you don't get bogged down in technical jargon and extraneous features and apps. In just six, short lessons, you'll learn how to:

- Quickly Navigate and Use the iPad User Interface
- Set Up Mail, Calendar, and Contacts
- Create and Use Folders to Multitask and Manage Apps
- Add Files to Your iPad, and Sync Them
- View and Manage Pleadings, Case Law, Contracts, and other Legal Documents
- Use Your iPad to Take Notes and Create Documents
- Use Legal-Specific Apps at Trial or in Doing Research

30-DAY RISK-FREE ORDER FORM

Join the ABA Law Practice Division today and receive a substantial discount on Division publications!

Product Code:	Description:	Quantity:	Price:	Total Price:
				$
				$
				$
				$
				$

Shipping/Handling:			Subtotal:	$
$0.00 to $9.99	add $0.00	*Tax: IL residents add 9.25% DC residents add 6%	*Tax:	$
$10.00 to $49.99	add $6.95		**Shipping/Handling:	$
$50.00 to $99.99	add $8.95		Yes, I am an ABA member and would like to join the Law Practice Division today! (Add $50.00)	$
$100.00 to $199.99	add $10.95			
$200.00 to $499.99	add $13.95		Total:	$